D0746396

*Lost and Found Again*

*or*

# PIERRE CHOLET

*Pierre Cholet*

*Lost and Found Again*
*or*

# PIERRE CHOLET

J.-B. PROULX

*New translation and annotations*
*by J. R. Koenig*

New York, 2007

*This book is dedicated to the memory of*
*Carol C. Sholette, "Jake" (1923-2007)*

Translation with new notes, maps and illustrations
from the original, unabridged edition of
*L'Enfant perdu et retrouvé, ou, Pierre Cholet*
(Montreal: Institution des Sourds-Muets, 1887)

© 2007 by J. R. Koenig
All rights reserved.

ISBN 978-0-6151-5081-9

Cover design and art: J. R. Koenig

Frontis is from the 1926 edition of
*L'Enfant perdu et retrouvé, ou, Pierre Cholet*

# CONTENTS

*Translator's Note*    *vii*

1   *J.-B. Proulx's Preface*    *1*

2   *Kidnapped*    *13*

3   *My Captive Years*    *27*

4   *Gaining My Freedom*    *45*

5   *Reaching My Homeland*    *73*

6   *My Long Search*    *85*

7   *My Searches Stopped*    *121*

8   *Finding My Parents*    *133*

*Afterword*    *149*

# MAPS

Quebec, Maritimes and Newfoundland  *xiv*

St.-Polycarpe  *12*

St.-Polycarpe to St. Malo (1845)  *24*

French Shore  *32*

Two Shipwrecks  *37*

Two Desertions  *48*

Jersey  *53*

Black Bay to Matane (1870)  *72*

Matane to Montreal (1870)  *86*

Montreal to Morrisburg (1870-1874)  *93*

Morrisburg to Clarence (1874-1876)  *102*

Clarence to Cornwall (1876-1879)  *122*

# BOXED TEXTS

J.-B. Proulx  *9-11*

Shallop  *21*

Seigneury System  *23*

St. Malo: Cod and Corsair Capital  *28-29*

Ship's Boys  *31*

French Fisheries  *32*

Barque (Bark) & Steamer  *34-35*

Frigate  *46*

Jerseyans  *53*

*Métis* & Louis Riel  *68-69*

Micmac (Mi'kmaq) Nation  *79*

April Fool's Day/*Poisson d'Avril*  *107*

*Voyageurs*  *111-112*

Tanneries  *129*

# TRANSLATOR'S NOTE

This nineteenth century adventure story takes place on the high seas, in the port city of St. Malo, France, and in the rugged countryside and bustling urban centers of eastern Canada. It is a tale of one man's perseverance despite all obstacles and hardships to return home. It is also a true story; the real-life hero of our tale died 100 years ago this year, 2007.

The story begins in 1845 when three small boys, ages four, five and six, disappear from a farming community in southwestern Quebec. Families and neighbors soon organize a massive manhunt for them. Hundreds of volunteers fan out to comb the surrounding fields and forests and soon those of adjacent parishes as well. The intense search turns up no signs of the lost boys and is reluctantly abandoned. Thirty-six years later, only one of the lost boys, now a forty-one-year-old man, returns.

In 1886, Pierre Cholet wrote out the story of his thirty-six year odyssey. He took his manuscript to a book publisher in Montreal who promptly sent him to the author and priest Jean-Baptiste Proulx for a major rewrite.

Proulx listened to Cholet spin out episodes of his life seasoned with words and expressions unique to Quebec. Cholet told Proulx about his kidnapping, the fate of the two other boys, his hard life as a sailor on the high seas, his near death in Labrador's wilderness, and his decade of wanderings across eastern Canada in search for his parents. He related his fortunate and not so fortunate encounters with a variety of people from different cultures and walks of life: farmers, seal hunters, *voyageurs*, a Métis, a Micmac man, smallpox victims. Lastly, he described his emotional reunion with his parents who had long ago given him up for dead. Proulx combined his literary skills with Pierre's talents as a raconteur to produce this enthralling, true story.

The following year, Pierre Cholet's story appeared in Montreal bookstores under the title "L'Enfant perdu et retrouvé, ou, Pierre Cholet." A French Canadian's true story of survival and courage, it became instantly popular in Quebec. It was also one of the first Canadian books published in French for young readers. "Pierre Cholet" may also have benefited from the popularity of Longfellow's 1847 epic poem "Evangeline" about young lovers tragically separated as a result of the British expulsion of the Acadians in 1755 (see boxed text p. 68) and their lifelong search to find each other again. Judging by the fact that "Pierre Cholet" has been republished in French at least eighteen times, most recently in 2000, it has become something of a classic in francophone Canada.

In 1888, the original publisher brought out an English translation of the story. At that time, the English-speaking market was still sizeable in Montreal; in fact, from the 1830s to the 1860s the majority of Montreal's population was anglophone. As its title "Pierre Cholet, or, the Recovered Kidnapped Child" indicates, this translation was unfortunately perfunctory; its stilted English flattened Cholet's voice, leaving few traces of his ironic expressiveness. It also dispensed with all but four of Proulx's forty-six footnotes, many of which would have enriched the text and enhanced the anglophone reader's understanding of French Canadian life. That translation (which can be found on microfilm at the Library and Archives Canada) was never reprinted and until now no one since has published a new English translation.

My new translation is based on the original and most complete edition of 1887. I have made few structural changes and additions. Proulx's Preface has now become Chapter 1. There are two reasons for this: Proulx's Preface contains a lot of information important to the story, and the story is really the product of both Cholet's and Proulx's voices. To better orient the reader over the course of Cholet's thirty-six year odyssey, I have put the unfolding months and years that appear so regularly in the pages into the right hand running heads. To aid readers unfamiliar with the geography of eastern Canada, I have added new maps showing nearly all the towns and rivers mentioned (except for those I couldn't locate on current maps), as well as the routes Cholet followed in his ten year search, when he traveled several hundred miles across eastern Canada, mostly on foot, often in the dead of winter and well before the advent of automobiles and ski-doos. Unlike the first English translation, I retained about two thirds of Proulx's footnotes—his name appears at the end of each of his footnotes—omitting only those that contained little or no historical or cultural information.

Proulx explained at the end of what is now Chapter 1 that he wrote his footnotes in order to clarify French Canadian expressions for francophone readers unfamiliar with them. In his footnotes he pointed out the inventiveness of French Canadian expressions in describing unique conditions of Canadian life, whether they involved the usage of old French, the borrowing of English words, or the coining of new Canadianisms. In short, he wanted his footnotes also to convey, especially to non-Canadian readers, that new Canada was developing its own culture and a new vocabulary with which to express it. The reader who is patient enough to read all Proulx's footnotes included here may agree with me that he was also waging a gentle campaign to loosen Canadian French from the tight control of the ever-authoritative Académie française. King Louis XIII's Cardinal Richelieu institutionalized the Académie française in 1635—Richelieu also devised the seigneurial system of land distribution for the French colonists of New France (see boxed text p. 23). To this day, the Académie française has remained a powerful force in regulating the official French language in Canada as well as in France and in keeping Canadianisms (chiefly *québécismes*) out of standard French dictionaries published either in France or Canada. Proulx might seem to be campaigning in his footnotes for the inclusion of the Canadianisms he helped define.

Proulx's footnotes also demonstrated his consciousness of the weight of new Canada's colonial past and of its evolving social history. Besides an adventure story and a classic odyssey tale, this slim book also contains a compressed history of French Canadian life in the second half of the nineteenth century. To unpack some of this history for the reader, I have added to several of Proulx's footnotes and have provided a dozen new notes to explain terms or events that Proulx might have thought needed no explanation in his day such as Geneviève de Brabant, the Grand Trunk Railway, the *voyageurs*, and the ever present danger of smallpox. Longer notes with new illustrations appear in the pages as boxed texts (references to them are underlined in the text).

In the year of Pierre Cholet's birth, 1840, francophone Lower Canada (Quebec) and anglophone Upper Canada (Ontario) were unified into one Canadian province and in 1867 into separate provinces within the confederation of Canada. In Cholet's lifetime, railroad lines connecting eastern to western Canada and to cities in the United States were new or just beginning. Sailing vessels still competed with steamers on the high seas and cod, fished from Newfoundland's Grand Banks, was a major industry. *Voyageurs*, those hardy canoe men working for the fur companies still made their trips via waterways and portage over thousands of miles of Canada's interior. Priests like the author Jean-Baptiste Proulx continued to make trips by canoe to missions in the forests of Hudson's Bay. There were still frequent outbreaks of smallpox, that dreaded disease so devastating to all populations, and especially to First Nations people.

But if much of the above has vanished from the historical stage, there is much in Cholet's story that continues to resonate in the present. Today there seems to be renewed concern over the exploitation of casual, itinerant, or migrant labor (now called "precarious labor") in the third world as well as in the first. Pierre Cholet was such a precarious worker. He worked as a temporary farm and stable hand, and as a casual laborer in a phosphate mine, a lumber camp, a sawmill and textile mill—all places without safeguards against layoffs, sickness or injury, or even nonpayment of earned salary. He also worked for fifteen years as a merchant sailor, an occupation that remains highly dangerous and exploited around the world today. The language and cultural divides between anglophone and francophone Canadians have not disappeared, nor has the division between so-called standard French maintained by the Académie française and Quebec French. Indeed, it may have deepened since Proulx's and Cholet's time. Today a debate goes on in Quebec over the necessity or even desirability of producing a standard dictionary of Quebec French (though it is supposed to be published any year now). In Ristigouche, New Brunswick, where Cholet encountered a Micmac man, there is a Micmac reserve. As of 1998 when I toured that area, Labrador's Black Bay where Cholet jumped ship had no roads connecting it to the outside world, and it remained as Cholet described it in 1870: a desolate, rocky, moss-covered terrain with stands of stunted trees and patches of ataca and pembina berries. Many poor coastal communities in Labrador and Newfoundland still seemed to be waiting for the unlikely return of the primordial cod industry that so ensnared Pierre's and Toussaint's lives.

## ACKNOWLEDGEMENTS

I wish to thank several of Pierre Cholet's many relatives who have helped me with this book. The family name Cholet is today most commonly spelled Cholette, but many relatives in the United States use the spelling Sholette. My husband's parents Carol and Julia Sholette got me started on translating this book many years ago, when they asked me to translate the author's preface. Except for the preface, Carol's father Maguire (Magloire) Sholette had completed a translation of the book shortly before he died in 1975. Maguire was a great grandson of Pierre's half brother, Mathias Cholet. I am grateful for his translation. I consulted it frequently, though I largely departed from it. Jack Cholette generously made his excellent research into the family genealogy available to me. He cleared up several mysteries about Pierre Cholet's immediate family: he discovered who were Pierre's siblings in Ogdensburg, what happened to Pierre's wife and infant daughter, and where Pierre spent his final years. Pierre Cholet's great nephew Marcel Cholette of St.-Polycarpe and his wife Carmen, extended their warm hospitality to my family and me on our two visits to St.-Polycarpe; they showed us Pierre Cholet's old family homestead and farm, which their son (also named Pierre) now manages, and they generously provided me with copies of many useful family documents. Thanks go to Marcel Cormier of Blanc Sablon who told me about the existence of the old 1888 translation on microfilm and to the Bibliothèque et Archives nationales du Québec (BAnQ), which has made many of its archives accessible on the internet and has kindly given me permission to reprint images from three illustrated journals published at the end of the 19th century: *l'Opinion publique*, and its successors, *le Monde illustré* and *l'Album universel*. Thanks also go to David Stern who so generously gave a final proofreading of the pages. Lastly, my husband and daughter Greg and Ariana Sholette gave me help and encouragement beyond the beyond. They also gamely went with me in the summer of 1999 to St. Malo, France where Pierre was taken after he was kidnapped, and they traveled with me the previous summer through much of eastern Canada to retrace the routes Pierre Cholet followed in his ten years of wandering to find his family. We traveled around Newfoundland, up along the Labrador coast to Black Bay, around the Gaspé Peninsula to Ristigouche and Matane, westward along the scenic St. Lawrence River, spotting the towns along the river Pierre passed through, to Quebec city, to Montreal and, finally, to his birthplace in St.-Polycarpe, where a helpful and friendly local librarian introduced us to Marcel and Carmen Cholette.

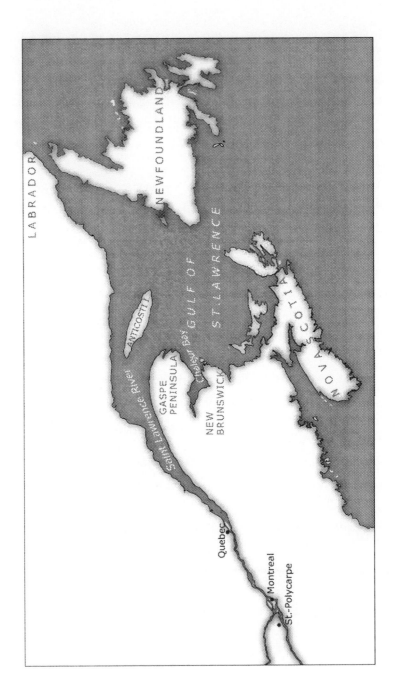

# 1

## *J.-B. Proulx's Preface*

*I*t was the beginning of February 1886. I was then the chaplain of the Sisters of the Good Shepherd's women's prison at 182 Fullum Street in downtown Montreal. A stranger introduced himself to me.

" Sir, they tell me that you write books."

"Sometimes."

"I was a lost child. I was born in the parish of St.-Polycarpe; my father's name is Hyacinthe Cholet. At the age of five I was kidnapped. I spent my boyhood at sea; when I was thirty I deserted ship. I began searching for my parents and after ten long years I found them. I wrote out the story of my life and took it to a book publisher. After taking a minute to look it over, the publisher told me quite frankly that my writing couldn't hold a reader's interest. He sent me to you. Could you fix it up for me?"

"My friend, leave your manuscript with me and come back in a few days; we'll see."

I saw that there was material for a completely original, little volume of adventures and stirring episodes— something along the lines of Geneviève de Brabant. But with this difference: Canon Schmid's[1] tale was only fiction, whereas Mr. Cholet's story was the pure and simple truth.

Meanwhile, on February 17th, I was appointed parish priest of Ile-Bizard.[2] The trouble and confusion of moving, the diverse preoccupations of a pastor's ministry, the additional obligations involved in the upcoming jubilee year,[3] and other literary work requiring my final touches—all this resulted in the notebook of the lost child gathering dust in the bottom of my bookshelf for several months. In November, I was able to study it a little. I soon discovered that the narrative sequence was riddled with holes and like bare bones devoid of flesh or marrow, a good many events had no framework or connective tissue. This is typical of the meager narratives that those with little writing experience produce. Perplexed about how to explain a detail, they skip over it. However, it is precisely in those carefully developed and organized details that one finds all the charm and interest.

1. Canon Schmid (Christoph von Schmid, 1768-1854) was a German priest, later canon of the Cathedral of Augsburg, who became a popular writer of children's stories, often with instructive morality lessons. One of his stories was based on a popular medieval tale of the triumph of innocence, Geneviève de Brabant. Falsely accused of infidelity, Geneviève went into hiding and suffered many adventures and hardships before her husband, the Duke of Bavaria, learned of her innocence and miraculously rescued her. Geneviève de Brabant also became a light opera by Jacques Offenbach in 1859.

2. Ile Bizard is the small island just north of Montreal; see map p. 12.

3. The jubilee year in 1887 was the 50th anniversary of Queen Victoria's reign; her long rule coincided with the height of the British Empire.

I had Mr. Cholet come by my office where he spent the next eight days. I interrogated him at great length. He told me all the phases of his troubled life. Gaps were filled in, events completed, obscure points clarified. When told from his lips rather than from his pen, his adventures took on a whole new life, one that was now animated and moving. Only then was I able to apply myself to editing his text at my own speed, with complete knowledge of the facts, and without being stopped at every turn by insoluble problems or incomplete accounts. When the work was finished in March of this year (1887) and before delivering a copy to the printer, I asked Mr. Cholet to come see me again. In one session, pen in hand, I read him the whole work and together we corrected a few small errors that had slipped in. Thus I can say, that apart from my footnotes, this book contains not a single invention of mine.

Everything about the hero of this story dispels the idea of a hoax: his candid and frank demeanor, his manners full of naive simplicity, and his natural shyness. There were no contradictions between the different sections of his story. I had visited St. Malo where he said he spent his childhood. I had passed by the coasts of Labrador and Chaleur Bay where he wandered for several months after his escape. Several times and without giving anything away, I subjected him to detailed questioning regarding the geographical and topological description of these regions. He passed all my tests with honor.

OVER THE SUMMER WHILE having gone to visit the pastor of St.-Polycarpe parish, I went to call on Mr. and Mrs. H. Cholet, who are still living; the father wasn't at home. I was struck by the resemblance between the mother and her son not only in the contours of the face, but in the color of the complexion, and especially in the timbre of the voice. This good mother is convinced that God in his mercy brought her child back. "No one in the whole family doubts it," she says. Her words and her explanation, as much about the kidnapping of little Pierre as about his return, agree perfectly with those set down in my notebook.

I got out the baptismal record of the child, Pierre Cholet, and found his age to be exactly that which Mr. Cholet gives himself. Here is the document in its entirety:

> This October 4th, 1840, we the undersigned priests have baptized Pierre, born the 28th of last month from the lawful marriage of Hyacinthe Cholet, local farmer, and Angélique André, known as St.-Amand. Godfather, Pierre André known as St.-Amand; godmother Justine Cholet who, as well as the father, were unable to pen their signatures. —T. BRASSARD, PRIEST.

I circulated a letter to fifteen or so completely trustworthy people who lived in Mr. Hyacinthe Cholet's vicinity at the time of the kidnapping. Their replies confirmed the statements of our hero. I present these letters in their charming simplicity.

> MR. HYACINTHE CHOLET: I, the undersigned Hyacinthe Cholet, father of Pierre Cholet the child who was lost and found again, certify that on the 7th of July 1845, Friday afternoon, my two sons Pierre and Toussaint together with Pierre Doucet, my cousin's little boy, disappeared from the house without my knowledge shortly after the visit of a peddler who, I believe, cast a spell over them. Right away we began to search for them with the neighbors' help. We searched everywhere without success. The following Sunday, Mr. Robert, then St.-Polycarpe's pastor, said only low Mass and called upon his parishioners to go looking for the lost children. More than five hundred people combed the woods for them. From time to time we heard the sad sound of the Church bell which served as our compass in

the forest to prevent us from getting lost ourselves. During the next fifteen days, searches went as far as Beauharnois and Châteauguay, always with no result. In the end we despaired of any success. That's when a sea of bitterness crashed down on us. Thirty-five years later, in September 1880, Pierre was found again. Upon that faith, I put my signature.

MRS. ANTOINE DOUCET, mother of Pierre Doucet who was taken at age six at the same time as Pierre Cholet, his second cousin: I certify that my son Pierre was lost in the same circumstances and was searched for with the same care as described in Mr. Hyacinthe Cholet's letter, which has just been read to me. It is needless to try to describe my suffering when this tragedy struck us. I remained inconsolable for thirty-five years. It has comforted me to learn from Mr. Pierre Cholet's own lips how my poor child died.

MR. ISAIE HAMELIN: I am one of those who went on the search when the children were lost. They went missing in the afternoon. As soon as I heard the news of their disappearance, I joined in the search with their parents. Everyone came from all sides to join in the search. The woods were big in those days. We positioned ourselves one beside the other at a distance of about five feet apart; then we went through the woods. Some of us had guns, which we fired from time to time; others carried megaphones. We heard cries all day long and throughout the night, too. We lit small fires from one place to the next; we went through the woods from one row of trees to another. At mealtimes, we ate in the local homes of wherever we happened to be. As soon as a meal was finished we left for another area, and this for fifteen days. If I have a good memory, it was forty-two years ago when this misfortune occurred. I found it so sad that I never forgot it.

MRS. ISAIE HAMELIN, SOPHIE CEDILOT: When the little children were lost I was staying at Mr. Hyacinthe Cholet's next-door neighbors. The whole time they lived with their parents I watched them growing up. They went missing in the afternoon; their mothers thought they had gone strawberry picking. A small tradesman had come around that day and Cholet's mother had bargained for some lace without having bought any. This made the tradesman angry; he said to her, "You will remember me." At first the mother didn't fret about her children's absence. But when evening came and they still hadn't returned, she began to worry. Antoine Doucet, the father of little Doucet who was lost with the two little Cholets, called over to me from his house, "Are the children with you?" I answered, "No." They used to come over almost every day. They began looking for them from house to house. No one had seen them. Antoine Doucet went to see his brother, Pierre Doucet, at Rivière à Delisle, thinking that they could have gone over there. He returned alone. The two mothers burst into tears and cried and cried. We went out with the other neighbors to begin looking for them. The same night, late in the evening, papa came back from the lake. Upon entering he said, "I don't know what's going on in the neighborhood, but everybody near and far is shouting at the top of their voices." We told him that the children were lost.

HONORÉ LAUZON: I, the undersigned, certify that upon the recommendation of Reverend Roux, St.-Joseph of Cèdres' pastor, I was part of said parish joining the search in the parish of St.-Polycarpe, at that time heavily wooded, for the three children who were lost: Pierre Cholet, Toussaint Cholet, and Pierre Doucet. That was in the month of July 1845.

MR. AUGUSTIN BELANGER: I certify that I myself had gone on the search for the children. I heard the church bell ringing the alarm. In our party, we were not less than two hundred men. The last time I saw the children, the day of their disappearance, all three of them were in the street having fun making mud pies in the sand. Pierre Giroux was with me.

Mr. Roger Duckett, Postmaster of Côteau-Station: I remember very well that in the year 1845 three little children by the name of Cholet and Doucet in Ste.-Marie hill, parish of St.-Polycarpe, were lost; that I heard the parish church bell ringing, no doubt calling everyone to join in the search, and that my father sent men to search with the others.

Antoine Giroux: I am an old man who has never left the area, and I have remained Mr. Hyacinthe Cholet's fourth neighbor. When the children were lost, we began searching on the south side; then we went to the north side of Sainte-Marie hill. More than four hundred people marching in a line, one person every four feet, took part in the search, which lasted over fifteen days.

Enough regarding citations; I could multiply them over and over again. I believe it comes out of the above evidence that this story is neither a fiction, a tale, a legend, nor even what is often called a historical novel, but very much the exact account of real events as they happened without any cosmetic alterations or embellishments. I was scrupulous not to add anything to the naked truth, nor to cut anything out. I didn't want to wring emotions from an over-excited imagination. The simple recounting of these sad adventures seemed to me sufficient for engaging the mind and touching the heart.

I left the words to the hero himself, confining myself to putting order and balance to the exposition, and to correcting the grammar. I believed I had to leave in his speech a certain number of Canadianisms. I hope the reader will thank me for not having edited out of the story this local color, this flavor of the Laurentian territory. Only for the edification of non-Canadians who wouldn't be able to grasp the nuances, have I given the explanation or the origin of these expressions in short footnotes.[4]

Dear reader, indulge me. For your enjoyment I have worked many nights without sleep. If you encounter a few errors in these pages, don't be too cross. An author likes to correct his book's pages as they come off the press. Now when mine are printed, I will be quite far from here, traveling with Monsignor Lorrain in the forest wilderness that covers the high country between Quebec Province and Hudson's Bay.

*Given at the church of St.-Raphael of Ile-Bizard, the 24th of May 1887, the golden anniversary of Queen Victoria, and the even more solemn holiday of Mary, Queen of Angels and Men: Auxilium christianorum, ora pro nobis.*
—J.-B. PROULX, PRIEST

4. Most of Proulx's footnotes, except for those that have little historical or cultural relevance, are retained in this translation with his name appearing at the end of his notes; see also Translator's Note, p. ix.

**Jean-Baptiste Proulx** (1846 -1904) was a priest, a professor of history and literature, and an author of several books, essays, plays and poems. He was also engaged with the social and political issues of his day.

Proulx studied classics and theology at the Seminary of St. Thérèse near Montreal and was ordained a priest in 1869. From 1871 to 1875 he served as a missionary in the new province of Manitoba. From 1877 to 1884 he was professor of history and literature at his old seminary where he threw his energies into rebuilding the seminary after a devastating fire in 1881, as well as into writing several plays for students, among them, "Edward the Confessor." From 1884 to 1886 he served as chaplain of the Asile St. Darie, a women's prison in downtown Montreal founded and run by the Sisters of the Good Shepherd, where he first met Pierre Cholet. Next he was appointed pastor of Ile Bizard and in 1888, pastor of St. Lin (see map p. 12) a position he held for the rest of his life.

While pastor of St. Lin, Proulx became embroiled in two important controversies requiring him to make several trips to the Vatican to plead his cause. The first concerned the future of the University of Laval's Montreal branch and its medical school; the second was the Manitoba school crisis of 1896. While still remaining pastor of St. Lin, Proulx also became Vice-Rector of the University of Laval at Montreal from 1889 to 1895. There, he found himself at the center of a conflict over the possible independence of the Montreal branch from its mother university, the University of Laval in Quebec City. In 1852, the University of Laval opened as the first French language Catholic university in Canada; in 1878 it opened its Montreal branch. According to Proulx's biographer Abbot Elie-J. Auclair*, the later successful independence of the Montreal branch, which became the University of Montreal in 1919, and the preservation of its medical school owed much to Proulx's under-recognized efforts. In 1896 Proulx became involved in the struggle over government funding of and the survival of French language public schools in Manitoba, when the English-speaking settlers moving into the area were greatly outnumbering the French-speaking inhabitants—a controversy that further exacerbated divisions between English and French Canadians. Against the opposition of his diocese, Proulx supported the liberal Prime Minister Laurier's compromise resolution of the Manitoba school crisis, which Pope Leo XIII later came to support.

Proulx traveled widely. He made two journeys to missions in the forests of Hudson's Bay with Monsignor Lorrain; he toured Europe with Pastor Labelle in order to attract French colonists; and he made several trips to Rome. He published books on his travels with Lorrain and Labelle and on the Manitoba school crisis,

"The canoe carrying Monsignor Lorrain [and Father J.-B. Proulx] into Indian territory in Hudson's Bay." *Le Monde illustré*, May 28, 1887. Courtesy of the Bibliothèque et Archives nationales du Québec (BAnQ hereafter).

as well as several pamphlets on his work as Vice-Rector of the future University of Montreal.

Throughout his life, Proulx took what he believed were principled positions regardless of the consequences on his career or his standing among the clergy.

When they met in 1886, Proulx was forty years old, six years Cholet's junior. Proulx died from a sudden illness in 1904 at the age of fifty-eight.

*Abbé Elie-J. Auclair, *Figures canadiennes. Première série*, (Montréal: Editions Albert Lévesque, 1933) 127-137
  See street named after Abbot Elie Auclair in St.-Polycarpe, detail map p.12.

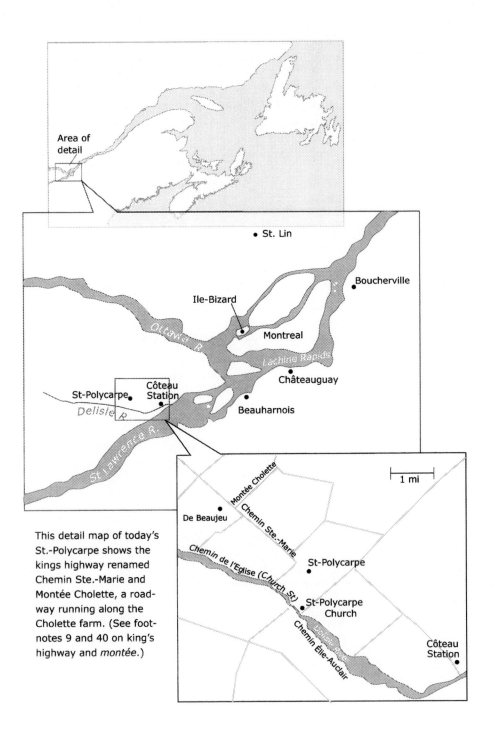

Area of detail

St. Lin

Boucherville

Ile-Bizard

Montreal

Ottawa R.

Lachine Rapids

Châteauguay

St-Polycarpe

Côteau Station

Delisle R.

Beauharnois

St Lawrence R.

This detail map of today's St.-Polycarpe shows the kings highway renamed Chemin Ste.-Marie and Montée Cholette, a roadway running along the Cholette farm. (See footnotes 9 and 40 on king's highway and *montée*.)

1 mi

Montée Cholette

De Beaujeu

Chemin Ste.-Marie

Chemin de l'Eglise (Church St.)

St-Polycarpe

St-Polycarpe Church

Chemin Élie-Auclair

Delisle River

Côteau Station

# 2

## *Kidnapped*

AT HOME

*M*y name is Pierre Cholet. I was born in 1840. My father's name is Hyacinthe Cholet and my mother's Marie St.-Amand. I saw the first light of day from Sainte-Marie hill (*côte Ste.-Marie*),[5] St.-Polycarpe, Soulanges County, about three miles from the church; our house was the second from the school.[6]

I was stolen at the age of five—or rather, to be exact, I was four years, nine months and twenty days old—along with my younger

---

5. "In the district of Montreal, the various concessions were called "*côtes*" [hills, hillsides], undoubtedly, because the first concessions of land were those on riverbanks or hillsides surrounding Mont Royal; from there, by analogy, the name was passed on to concessions more in the interior whether they were located on hillsides and riverbanks or not. One reads in the 'History of the French Colony in Canada' by M.Rallon, Vol. III, p. 222: 'As soon as it became known that the troops were at sea, many went to establish land rights on land

brother Toussaint Cholet who was a little over three years old, and my cousin Pierre Doucet, aged six. I can recall the details of the kidnapping as if it were yesterday; I thought about it so often while I was on foreign land.

It happened in the summer, on July 7th, 1845, so I've since been told. My brother and I had come back to the house from picking raspberries outside. It must have been around ten o'clock in the morning. I demanded a buttered muffin from my mother who was busy walking about the house carrying something in her arms. She told me to wait a bit. I continued my whining demands. She gave me a slap, with the words, "Go away then, little pest."[7]

I got angry, took off my little raincoat (*bougrine*)[8] and threw it on the ground saying, "Fine, I'm going away and never coming back."

---

not yet claimed, some above the town and others beyond the Saint Peters River, on the banks of the St. Lawrence. These properties began to be designated in City Hall by the name *côtes* and the *côtes* were distinguished one from the other by Saints' names.'"—J.-B. Proulx

Today in St.-Polycarpe, the name *côte Ste.-Marie* (Ste.-Marie hill) is no longer in use. The name Sainte-Marie is now applied only to the old king's highway, the road (*chemin*) running along the old Sainte-Marie hill.

6. Before the 1840s there were few schools for rural families, which is why Pierre's father, for example, was unable to read or write. After the Act of Union of 1840 uniting Upper and Lower Canada (today's Ontario and Quebec) and subsequent legislation to establish a school system of separate primary and normal schools for Catholics and Protestants, many new parish schools opened. While in 1842 there were only about 3000 French Catholic students, by 1855 there were 127,000 ("Catholic Encyclopedia (1913) Catholicity in Canada"<http://en.wikisource.org/wiki/Catholic_Encyclopedia_%281913%29/Catholicity_in_Canada?oldid=338370>)

7. "It's not without interest to recount this little incident. Like any tenderhearted mother who often went to great pains for her children, Pierre's mother bitterly reproached herself after the kidnapping for this little slap that led to her child's prank. She never spoke of this incident to anyone, not even

LOOKING FOR
RASPBERRIES

I looked out the window to watch out for my cousin, who lived across the road from us. He came out his door and I joined him.

"Wait for me, wait for me!" my little brother Toussaint cried running after us..

We stopped. He had managed to get a buttered muffin and gave us each a bite. We set off. At first we followed the king's highway[9] in order to go eat raspberries on a neighbor's property, the second farm from Mr. Doucet's. Then we wandered along the boundary fence that ran westward towards the properties on the Delisle River. At that time, the parish was not cleared as it is now. Not too far from the houses you would see thick underbrush with stumps and felled trees half burnt and blackened. I remember that for quite some time we kept ourselves busy snapping off pussy willow branches. We were about to play on the banks of a creek when we saw a man approaching; he had a suitcase strapped to his back. We started to run away. He shouted at us to stop.

---

to her husband, instead, burying her sorrow in the bottom of her heart. Thirty years later, when Pierre returned and recalled this incident, this was strong proof of his identity. If he wasn't her child, how could he have guessed at this?" —J.-B. Proulx

8. "In Canada, one uses the word *bougrine*, in almost the same sense as redingote [top coat, old Eng. riding coat]. Without doubt, it comes from *bougran*, a strong, oil-cloth or oilskin [cloth made waterproof with oil] which would have been used to make this kind of apparel." —J.-B. Proulx

9. "The major roadways, which in France bear the names national, departmental or communal roads, in Canada are called king's highways; this is an expression that comes to us straight from the time of French rule, when the king could say, '*L'etat, c'est moi* [I am the state].'"—J.-B. Proulx

"Hey kids, where are you going?"

"We are playing, Sir."

"Come over here, so I can show you some toys (*bebelles*)."[10]

We were afraid and looked at each other anxiously. Then as if suddenly reassured we said, "Let's go see the box he has on his back."

He put his suitcase on the ground and had us examine his toys. "Now come over to my wagon and I will show you something even more beautiful."

We walked on a good bit. Pierre Doucet and I were happily holding the man's hands; Toussaint, miserable at trying to keep up with us, was crying.

There was a large box on top of the wagon like those found on peddlers' or bakers' wagons. At the front of the box behind the horse, sat an old lady and a girl around six years old.

"Get in," said the tradesman, "I will take you to your parents."

We didn't want to. We were crying. But he swept us up in his arms and forced us onto the wagon.

"It's a long way to our house," said Pierre Doucet.

"Yes, yes. Why don't you sleep until we get there?"

"No, we want to get down. Put us on the ground!"

Toussaint was crying his head off. In a rage, the tradesman stopped his horse short and unleashed a storm of curses, which was practically buffeting (*bourassant*)[11] us like a gust of heavy wind. He stuffed us inside the big box that we discovered contained only rags and scrap-iron. Then he cracked his whip and the horse took off at a gallop causing us to knock our heads violently against

---

10. "*Bebelles* [toys, gewgaws] isn't French but it should be. It is a child's repetition of *beau, bel*, like *joujou* is of *jou* [game] or *jouer* [to play]." —J.-B. Proulx

11. "Canadian word *bourassant*, which comes from *bourrasque*, a sudden gust of wind that lasts only a moment; and figuratively, a short burst of temper." —J.-B. Proulx

Peddler in Montreal. *L'Album universel*, 29 juillet 1905. Courtesy of BAnQ.

the sides of the box. Toussaint nevertheless soon fell asleep while Pierre Doucet and I cried the whole way.

Who stole us? That morning a peddler had come around in a wagon like the one I have just described. Madame Doucet, Pierre's mother, who was at our house at the time, as a tease[12] cajoled him into spreading out his merchandise; then she declared that she had no need of any of it. This made the man furious and the women laughed.

He told them, "You will remember me before this day is over."

Could it be that having spotted us kids roaming around our house he chose us as the victims of his vengeance? It's probable.

Had we been stolen from Ste.-Marie hill where our parents lived? While playing outside, had we followed the boundary fence along the length of the two lands, around sixty *arpents*,[13] as far as the Delisle River? What time was it when the tradesman carried

12. *"Etrivation*, a teasing for fun, from an old term *estriver* meaning to quarrel or squabble: 'With your neighbors day and night, squabbling [*estriver*],' Regnier, sat. XIII— 'Thus they began to squabble [*estriver*] among themselves,' an author from the XII century." —J.-B. Proulx

13. Fifty acres. An old unit of land measure in French Canada and Louisiana, one *arpent* equals about 5/6s of an acre or in linear distance about 190 feet or roughly sixty yards.

us off in his wagon? There are so many such questions that my poor memory cannot answer. I can only say that it was a very long time since we had left the house and that we had walked a good distance.


ON AN ISLAND

We traveled the rest of the day and night without stopping. At daybreak, we got off at a deserted riverbank. We were very hungry.

The tradesman put me in a canoe saying, "Be very still, while I go fetch your companions in the wagon."

Doucet was yelling, "Pierre, where are you? Where are you, Pierre?"

I answered him tearfully, "Where are our parents?"

The tradesman said menacingly, "Shut up, shut up at once."

Doucet started crying all the louder. The man hit Doucet on the head. "Shut up, that's enough useless crying."

Doucet quieted down for a moment.

I said to my brother, "Don't cry or the man will hit you."

He stopped crying but sighed for a long time. The three of us lay down on the bottom of the canoe with the woman and girl crouched in front and the man in back.

"Be calm," he said, "we're getting to your parents."

"Home?" asked Doucet.

"Yes, to your homes."

"It's a very long way," I replied.

No sooner did I raise my head a little bit (*un petit brin*)[14] to look around, than the tradesman growled, "Stay down!"

14. "*Brin* [a blade of grass, a wisp of straw, a crumb, a tiny bit of something], in Canada, is often used in the sense of little; and here the Canadians are only imitating Madame de Sévigné who used to say, 'I sometimes want you to have a little scrap [*un petit brin*] of these leftovers.'" —J.-B. Proulx

We reached a small island with its shores covered in under-brush, reeds and tall grasses. We spent three or four days there in a tent in the company of the old woman and the girl while the man was away. We slept on a buffalo skin[15]; the woman cooked outside on a stone hearth; we went around gathering pieces of wood to feed the fire. Unaware of our predicament, we even began to enjoy ourselves.

Now I ask myself, where could this island have been located? Was it at the foot of the Lachine Rapids? Was it at the base of the island of Montreal near Boucherville? In our nonstop voyage from the afternoon through the night, we could have reached one or the other place. All I can remember is that the island wasn't very big, there were no high trees, and the mainland looked very far away.

ON A SHIP

It was dark when the tradesman returned. He took us by canoe across the water and had us get off at a deserted beach without the woman and the girl. We wanted to gather shells but he brusquely stopped us. He put Toussaint up on a horse near its neck and took Pierre Doucet and me by the hand. Doucet started to cry.

The man stopped. "Are you going to stop crying? Yes or no?"

Pierre Doucet stopped for two or three minutes and then start-ed crying even louder than before.

"Either you're going to stop crying or you're really going to have something to cry about," said the tradesman.

He put Toussaint back on the ground, ran to find a switch, and gave Doucet three or four blows across the back.

15. "Buffalo skin is the tanned hide of the buffalo of the prairies with the hair left on." —J.-B. Proulx

"Shut up, you're not being reasonable."

The man took us to a house where there was only a woman and where we were to spend the night. She gave us some supper. Doucet ate only a few mouthfuls, saying he was sick. But my brother and I had good appetites. Being younger, we were less aware of our calamity than our cousin.

The next morning the tradesman came to see us accompanied by two large men. They looked us over without saying a word. We were scared. They returned that same night and made each of us put on blue clothing. The tradesman told us to follow the two men from now on. He had delivered his merchandise; he had sold us!

The two men led us to a <u>shallop</u> manned by five sailors. The night was as dark as a wolf's lair[16] and it was raining hard. After having sailed a good while, we climbed aboard a large vessel that had about fifty men on board.

The ship's captain was quite old; his beard was completely white. He made us stay in his cabin and questioned us at great length about our mother and father, and other relatives.

Doucet was crying and he told him, "Stop crying, and I will give you apples and candy."

My cousin kept quiet for the rest of the night. The captain's son, who was first mate, asked us our names. He said to Pierre Doucet, "From now on your name is Pierre Marin;" to me, "Your name is not Pierre anymore but Louis, Louis Marin;" and to Toussaint, "Your name is Toussaint Marin."

How well I now remember this event when he assigned new names to us, the names by which we then became known. Liv-

16. dark as a wolf's lair (*noir comme chez le loup*): "I haven't found this expression in the dictionary, but it seems very rational to me, because there could hardly be much light in a wolf's den."—J.-B. Proulx

The **shallop** (Fr. *chaloupe*) was a large, heavy rowboat or lifeboat that might be fitted with sail and could carry up to twelve people. The 19th century ocean sailing vessel usually carried two or more shallops. In the 1870s the smaller and lighter two-person dory began replacing the shallop.

Illus.: *L'Album universel*, 7 March 1903. Courtesy of BAnQ.

ing among strangers, we forgot our real names. It wasn't until many years later that I discovered that my real last name was Cholet and my cousin's, Doucet.

## DESPERATE SEARCHES

Let us return for a moment to my family's home and consider what happened. Of course, I only learned these details after my return to Saint-Polycarpe, when I had found my parents.

Our mothers didn't notice our absence until the afternoon. They first ran to all the neighbors and were surprised not to find us there. Some neighbors knew nothing about our comings and goings; others had seen us playing in the road making mud pies. That was all. Pierre Doucet's father headed off into the sunset over the Delisle River towards his brother's, thinking we could have walked that far. He returned discouraged. Without wasting any more time, the two families with some neighbors' help began scouring the woods in the surrounding area. They spent the entire night and the next day, which was Saturday, searching, calling, shouting, but in vain.

That Sunday, the Pastor of Saint-Polycarpe Father Robert said but one Low Mass. He announced that there would be no vespers that day and invited the whole parish to join the parents in the search. Father Roux of Cèdres made the same call to his parishioners. Hundreds of people gathered in Ste.-Marie hill. First they combed the fields and woods extending south towards the Delisle River and then those to the north towards Monsieur de Beaujeu's estate.

Like an army going into battle, the troops advanced in a single line, each person standing about four or five feet from his or her nearest neighbor, so that not a single path was left unbeaten, not a hiding place overlooked, not a thicket unexamined. The church bell kept ringing continually to signal to us, the lost children—if we were still alive—and also to prevent the searchers from getting lost themselves in the woods, which at that time were vast. Some fired rifles, others used megaphones; there was a continual hue and cry that echoed from one end of the parish to the other.

The search continued for fifteen days and in the neighboring parishes as well. At first everyone was anxious to find us alive. Then when that hope faded, they would have been happy to find our lifeless bodies, in order to bury us in consecrated ground and end our parents' anxiety. Our mothers were especially inconsolable. "If they had breathed their last," they said from their beds, "we could more easily submit to God's will. Did they die after

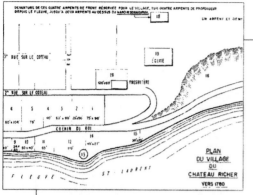

PLAN
DU VILLAGE
DU
CHATEAU RICHER
VERS 1780

This map of Château-Richer, the first rural parish in New France, shows the town evolving from the seigneury. Illus.(detail) from Raymond Gariépy, "Le Village du Château-Richer (1640-1870)," *Cahiers d'histoire,* No. 21 (Quebec: La Société historique de Québec, 1969) 155.

**Seigneurial System**

"One calls an estate the part of the seigneury that belongs exclusively to the seigneur [lord of the manor]."
—J.-B. Proulx

De Beaujeu was one of the seigneurs, in this area.

In the early 1600s, King Louis XIII's chief minister Cardinal Richelieu devised the seigneurial system to distribute land along the St. Lawrence River to French colonists. In this quasi-feudal system, France would give large land grants to individual entrepreneurs (be they nobles or commoners) who would guarantee to populate and cultivate the land within a determined period or else the land grants reverted back to the crown. These seigneurs would contract men to clear the land and build houses, forts, and mills. The seigneur would later sell or distribute parcels of the seigneury to these hired men at the end of their contract. "A typical seigneury measured 1 x 3 leagues [3 x 9 miles] and was divided into long narrow lots facing the river."*

*Canada Hall, Canadian Museum of Civilization Corporation, 2001.

being tortured? Were they devoured by wolves? Did they become food for birds of prey? This cruel uncertainty is crushing us."

They could never blot out this pain from their memory. Many long years later when I, alone, of the three children returned to my birthplace, I found that this wound was still fresh in their hearts.

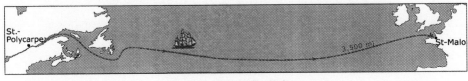

St.-Polycarpe to St. Malo

CROSSING THE OCEAN

We were on a course for France. We probably stopped for a few weeks in the Gulf of St. Lawrence, where the vessel we were on had some business connected with the fisheries.[17]

Oblivious to the seriousness of our troubles, my brother and I were again in good spirits. But Pierre Doucet was not eating and soon was dangerously ill. He languished a few days in his hammock, and after a short agony he died.

The first mate said to us, "Come watch us bury your companion at sea."

They placed him on a long plank and let him slide into the water; Pierre Doucet disappeared under the waves forever! I held my brother's hand and wept.

"Be quiet," said the first mate, "or we'll do the same to you."

The captain called us to his cabin and gave us candy to cheer us up. One is easily consoled at age five. From then on, I forgot my young friend. But several years later when my reasoning was more developed, his image resurfaced in my memory and I mourned for him. What I would give today to see him share in my good fortune!

The old captain heaped lots of toys and games on us; he often played with us. He enjoyed our company and was like a father to us. But the first mate was very harsh; when the captain was asleep, he would box our heads and pull our ears.

17. On fisheries, see boxed text p. 32.

One day the captain, his father, caught him bullying us and said, "Stop it, what harm have they done you?"

"They were dragging everything around on deck."

"So? You did the very same thing when you were small."

Then it was the good captain's turn to become ill. News spread that he was going to die. Everyone on board was anxious and upset and gave one another questioning looks. The sailors spoke quietly among themselves.

The captain called his son to his bedside and said, "God is calling me to him, take good care of the two little boys, don't mistreat them." He gave him many more instructions concerning us.

He had me come closer.

"Louis, I have something to tell you. You ought to know that I am not your father. If you don't know it, I will tell you because you can understand better than your little brother. There was a man whom I didn't know who stole you, who brought you to me and sold you. I was sorry for all of you. I hope God will not make me suffer too much for this act; I didn't steal you. Come closer, dear Louis, so I can embrace you. Take good care of your brother, mind the first mate and be a good boy. You too, Toussaint, come embrace me."

He wept and we wept with him.

A few days later the captain died. His body was taken to St. Malo, France where he had lived. We missed him a great deal. He had been kind and gentle to us little orphans. May God have mercy on his soul!

# 3

## *My Captive Years*

MY

EDUCATION

$M$y brother and I spent our childhood in <u>St. Malo.</u> We were housed with an old man named Mr. Cottin. This was the brother of the captain who had died at sea and uncle of the first mate who had become a captain in his father's place. Cottin's residence faced the wharves, which were located outside the town walls. We lived with him for eight or nine years. He was pretty good to us while his old wife was not at all.

Mr. Cottin ran a school for twenty or so boys. Seven or eight boys belonged, like ourselves, to the company and lived in his house. The others were children of the ships' officers. They lived elsewhere and we saw them only during class time. We were always under watch. We were never allowed out of the courtyard where we played except to go on company ships when they were

Côte d'Emeraude    1483.  SAINT-MALO — Le Casino et coin du Bassin
The Casino and a corner of the dock

St. Malo Postcards c. 1900

## St. Malo, Cod and Corsair capital

In the 1800s, St. Malo was the principal European port of the important cod trade. As early as the sixteenth century, fishermen routinely sailed from St. Malo to fish for cod along Newfoundland's coasts. In 1534, explorer Jacques Cartier of St. Malo became known as the first European to discover the St. Lawrence River.

St. Malo harbored many pirates and corsairs over the centuries. Corsairs or privateers were independent captains, also called "gentlemen pirates", who, with the support of their government, preyed upon merchant ships of rival countries. The famous corsairs René Duguay-Trouin in the late 1600s and Robert Surcouf, a hundred years later during the Napoleonic Wars, resided in St. Malo. France ennobled Duguay-Truoin and Surcouf who both so successfully plundered English ships and brought much wealth to St. Malo and the crown. England employed and ennobled her own corsairs, like Sir Francis Drake.

Robert Surcouf

Proulx visited St. Malo in 1885 and found statues to Cartier, Duguay-Trouin, Surcouf, and another former sea captain, the famous writer Chateaubriand, gracing the city. Malouins were proud of these famous residents and happy to point out to Proulx the houses where they once lived. Proulx observed that women were very much part of St. Malo's commercial life; "Like at Tyr, like at Carthage," he wrote, "wherever you find commercial people, you find women tending the counters."* He thought that the city could barely contain within its walls its population of 12,000. He discovered he could tour the entire city in thirty minutes from its ramparts. Built in the early 1600s, these impressive ramparts were 80% destroyed in World War II but completely restored since then using many of the old stones.

*J.-B. Proulx, *Cinq mois en Europe ou voyage du curé Labelle en France en faveur de la colonisation* (Montreal: Beauchemin & Fils, 1888) 79-80.

St. Malo ramparts
c. 1900

in port; then, we often had our meals there and slept on board. In those eight years, I went to town—though it was but a few steps away—only twice and always in the custody of Mr. Cottin. From time to time, the captain came to see us to inquire about our health and our progress in school.

Besides reading, I learned some spelling, arithmetic, geography, and my catechism at school. I made my First Communion aboard a company steamer where there was a chaplain named Arpin. We sometimes heard Mass on a ship's deck, but never in the town's churches. In reality we were prisoners. We already knew we had been kidnapped as children. From certain words that slipped out here and there, we learned from our captors that our parents lived in Canada. However, neither then nor later did we dare broach this subject with the captain, knowing that it would be extremely unwelcome.

MY FIRST SHIPWRECK

When we were older, myself fourteen or fifteen years old, my brother thirteen or fourteen, we embarked upon the first of our many ocean voyages, and, consequently, upon harnessing ourselves to a life of drudgery and misery. The work was even harder for my younger brother who was not as strong as I was and not as used to hard knocks; for in the beginning of our life on the high seas, we tasted more beatings than bread. Polish the knives, wash the dishes, wax the boots, swab the decks, climb the rigging—those were our daily chores. We shed enough tears to fill a small fountain.

The company owned a great number of vessels that it rented out: some to the government for troop transport, some to merchants for shipment of goods, others to associations of cod fisher-

COTES DE FRANCE

2332 — La Soupe du Matin

**Ship's boys**

(Fr. Mousses)

From the 1750s onwards, France required a steady supply of seasoned sailors to continue its endless competition with England for domination of the seas, and to maintain its fisheries. To that end, the French government began requiring its ship companies to place ship's boys (*mousses*) and novice sailors on every vessel and to maintain schools for training young sailors, such as the one Pierre and his brother attended in St. Malo.

The apprenticeship of a ship's boy was grueling and beatings were commonplace. Typical chores were loading and unloading provisions, preparing and serving coffee and food, cleaning the decks and the crew's cabins, unloading the catch; tarring the ship's hulls, and learning to repair nets and sails. The boys were completely dependent upon the good will of their captain to protect them from hardships on board and excessive abuse from the crew. As hard as shipboard life was in general, it was especially harsh and occasionally fatal on the cod ships (*terres-nuevas*). For that reason, many of those ship's boys were obtained from orphanages.[*]

[*] Nelson Cazeils, *Les Gens de Mer* (Rennes: Editions Ouest-France, 1996) 71, 76, 77; "Saint-Malo et la Grande Peche," 8.

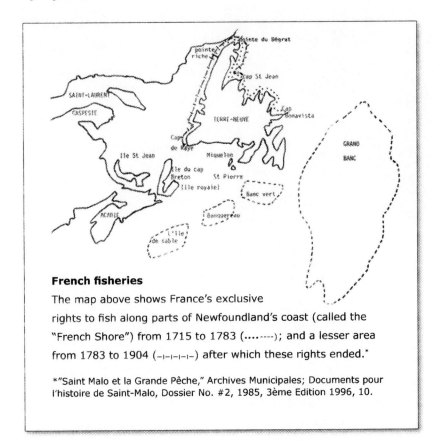

**French fisheries**

The map above shows France's exclusive rights to fish along parts of Newfoundland's coast (called the "French Shore") from 1715 to 1783 (.........----); and a lesser area from 1783 to 1904 (–ı–ı–ı–ı–) after which these rights ended.*

*"Saint Malo et la Grande Pêche," Archives Municipales; Documents pour l'histoire de Saint-Malo, Dossier No. #2, 1985, 3ème Edition 1996, 10.

men. Ours, loaded with provisions and fishing nets, was to supply and watch over the <u>French fisheries</u> near the coasts of Newfoundland. Our vessel was supposed to remove American and Nova Scotian vessels from French waters in order to prevent their poaching capelin,[18] a small fish used in making fodder. At our departure, there was a lot of cheering and waving from land, and from on

18. Capelin has other important uses besides fodder: it attracts cod, which feed on it, and it is used for fertilizer. Today like cod, capelin has been over fished in Newfoundland to the extent that it is unlikely to return to its former abundance (see Mark Kurlansky, *Cod: A Biography of the Fish That Changed the World* (New York: Walker Publishing Co., 1997) 5, 183).

board much firing of cannon. It was the first of April. Around the seventeenth of April, only a short distance from Pictou, we got caught in a big snowstorm accompanied by a severe wind from the southwest. We were on the verge of being shipwrecked.

The captain called to all hands, "Strike the sails!"

No sooner said than done, but it was too late. The vessel had struck a reef; we could hear the whole ship breaking up! The captain lamented to all the Saints; he so much wanted to save his crew. All around could be heard the cries, "We're going to die, we're going to die!" Several men with cork life belts on jumped overboard.

The five shallops were put afloat. The first one ready to leave carried twelve men; they all perished in the waves crashing over them.

The captain said to me, "Get in with me."

A sailor had to yell over and over again to Toussaint, "Hurry-up, hurry-up!" The poor kid, moaning all the while, leaped headlong into the shallop. The waves rose up as high as mountains; we rowed with all our might. We were about two hundred yards from land when a long, powerful wave lifted us and in one thrust carried us to shore; we jumped into water up to our waists. All of us pulling together, we managed to drag our boat up on the beach. By the grace of God, the other shallops also landed without mishap. There we were, shivering on a desolate coast, far from any settlement.

Of the fifty-five-man crew, forty-three survived; twelve bodies floated along the shoreline. We sadly retrieved our drowned comrades. They were unrecognizable: noses missing, bodies battered against the sharp rocks and mutilated. It was a ghastly sight. We had a lot of trouble burying those men. To dig the graves, we had to tear away clods of earth with pointed sticks and our bare hands. We were trembling all over from the cold wind and felt broken-hearted.

This painful task accomplished, the captain said to us, "Let's see if we can find some kind of building in the area."

Just as eight men jumped into a shallop we saw a ship rounding a point. "Quick, quick," shouted the captain, "try to meet it!"

We signaled furiously. The ship noticed us and turned towards us.

"Could you give me and my crew passage?" our captain asked. "We were shipwrecked in this morning's storm and thrown on this coast without any provisions."

"Gladly," said the captain whose name was Duquet. "But we are short on food, so you will be obliged to go on rations."

During our nine days on board, we got only a couple of ounces of salted beef each night. But in everything else we were treated generously. Captain Duquet was from Quebec. The following year, during a voyage he was making to Brazil with a cargo of dried codfish, his vessel sank with all aboard. May God reward him for his charity towards us!

**Barque** (or Bark)
The wooden, three-masted barque was the most common sea-going cargo-carrier in the mid 19th century. The two forward masts were square-rigged and the third, stern-most mast (mizzenmast) was fore-and-aft-rigged.*

*Amy Hand, *Golden Age of Sail* (N.Y.: Smithmark, 1996) 23.

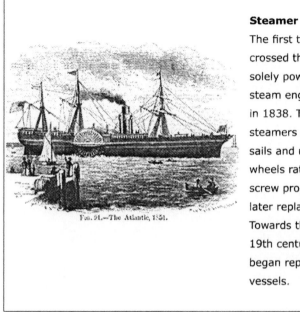

Fig. 31.—The Atlantic, 1851.

**Steamer**
The first time a vessel crossed the Atlantic solely powered by steam engine was in 1838. The early steamers also carried sails and used paddle wheels rather than the screw propellers that later replaced them. Towards the end of the 19th century, steamers began replacing sailing vessels.

On the tenth day, we encountered in mid-ocean a British vessel bound for Boston. We transferred from the <u>barque</u> to the <u>steamer</u> where, surrounded by an abundance of everything, we felt almost like wedding guests. We were set ashore in St. John's, Newfoundland where we took a French vessel to St. Malo. As you can see, my first voyage was not a pleasure trip; it was a bad omen.

MY MANY VOYAGES
Captain Cottin enrolled Toussaint at a boarding school in St. Malo. Toussaint was still too weak for work on ship and somewhat sickly. I am not a big man; I measure five feet, seven inches. Toussaint

was shorter than I, but heavier and stockier. He spent three years in college and left with a good education.

As for me, I shipped off for China. I always served under Captain Cottin on company ships, like the rest of the crew. This time we carried a shipment of dry goods and liquor to China and returned with a cargo of tea. Not a day passed that I did not think of Toussaint who had been my inseparable companion since childhood. Each night, I went to bed late and shed a tear remembering our good times together. By day, the pleasant memories gave way to work. I had to practice target shooting with the other sailors; I was one of the shallops' crew and, whenever there was any danger of attack, I was sure to be called into action.[19]

For ten years or so, always under Captain Cottin, I made many voyages: to Jamaica where we brought flour and returned with sugar and molasses; to Brazil, with shiploads of fish; along the coasts of Newfoundland and Labrador, guarding the French fisheries; to Boston and Portland in the United States; to Liverpool, England; to Bordeaux and LaRochelle, France. After his three years at school, Toussaint joined me to share in my joys and my sorrows.

19. "one of the shallop crew: *l'homme de chaloupe*"
Shallops (large rowboats often fitted with sail, see text box, p. 21) were also deployed to defend the vessel during an attack. An ocean-going merchant vessel plying the trade between St. Malo and Newfoundland might carry a crew of forty to fifty men that included eighteen or so sailors to man the shallops.

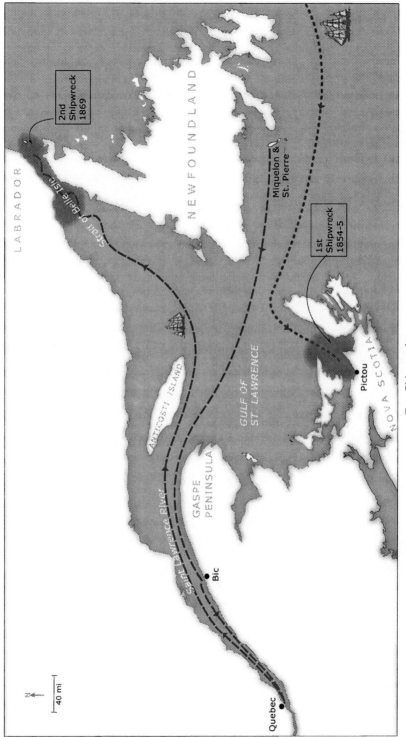

Two Shipwrecks

## MY SECOND
## SHIPWRECK

In autumn 1869, we embarked from St.-Pierre and Miquelon[20] for Quebec with a shipload of fish. Besides Captain Cottin and the first mate, there were only thirteen sailors aboard. At Bic, we picked up a pilot. As the wind was good, he had us spread all our sails. It must have been about seven in the evening. The next morning we dropped anchor at the Quai des Indes.*

Since it was late in the season, we unloaded and reloaded quickly; our new cargo was lumber: planks and beams. We left on November 1st, All Saints Day. I had come so close to my home-land and now I was going away without any hope of returning. Toussaint and I had a vague premonition that our parents lived in the area and this thought left us feeling sad and empty.

A trade wind was blowing from the southwest. The yardarms carried all our sails and we had a good run down to the place where we put the pilot ashore. Three days later the wind changed; turning at mid-day it brought in a great snowstorm. It was impossible to pass to the south of Newfoundland. For better or worse, we had to enter the Strait of Belle Isle. The more the wind blew the harder it snowed. We hardly made any headway. That night the captain told the first mate to take in all of the sail save that necessary for steer-ing. We spent the entire night unable to grab a wink of sleep. The next morning there was a foot of snow on deck; the halyards, stiff and inflexible, were covered with a half-inch of ice. What misery we had handling the ship. Towards four in the afternoon, the wind slanted towards the southwest.

* Could not locate "Quai des Indes" on current maps.

20. The islands of St. Pierre and Miquelon are the only remaining French possessions in North America today.

The captain paced the poop deck with his hands in his pockets and scanned the horizon anxiously. "The day ends, night comes, the current takes us. I don't know where I am; our compasses are not working. If only the Blessed Virgin would allow me to see the sun for just one hour, we could be saved. But no, the storm worsens. What will become of us?"[21]

We were very discouraged. Toussaint was at the bow keeping watch. All at once he shouted, "I can see a dark mass, very close!"

The first mate ran over. "We're running aground!"

The captain was beside himself. "Oh! This is just what I feared!"

At that very moment the vessel rose up onto a huge rock and burst apart, cracked through the middle; it half filled with water but remained stuck on the reef. We had run aground on a rocky reef several hundred feet in circumference. Working furiously, we were able to save one of the shallops and get it into the water; it must have been around midnight. Snow was falling by the bucketful and waves as high as hills continued to roll in. The captain told us to wait until daylight before trying for land. We spent a bad night, always outside in the vile weather, half-frozen and shivering under squalls of wet snow that whipped about our faces.

The next morning, the snow continued, but the wind hardly

21. Nineteenth century captains had relatively few navigational aids: the notoriously unreliable maritime charts, the chronometer for calculating longitude, the magnetic compass, and the sextant, which calculated latitude by finding the angle between the horizon and a celestial body. From the captain's remarks, it seems he wanted to use his sextant but couldn't because of the storm.

blew, and the sea was calmer. The first mate left with nine sailors to reach the shore that we had seen at a distance of twenty-five or thirty miles. The shallop could carry no more men. Five of us remained onboard: the captain, my brother and I, and two other sailors, Asselin and Sansterre.

"As soon as you reach a settlement, send help."

"Yes, yes, good-bye."

"Bon voyage, good luck!"

It was a sad parting for we had a foreboding that we would never see each other again.

An hour after they left, the wind backed to the northeast with a vengeance. The water was whipped into a fine hard spray like the powdery snows[22] of winter and the snow fell so thickly that we could see no more than three feet in front of us. Minute by minute we watched to see if our men were ever coming back. The day ended, night passed, and still no one returned. The captain, pensive and depressed, began to weep; at this sight we began weeping with him. It was not a happy time.

The next day, the weather was beautiful: the water calm, the sun dazzling; we could see out over the water as far as the eye can see. But the whole day long, no one came back.

The captain said, "It looks very much like the rest of the crew is finished, all we can do now is pray for their souls."

22. "When the wind whips the snow into a fine powder, the Canadians say that it powders [*il poudre*]. This expression came to life with the Canadian people; indeed can you find me a better one? Since 1696, Father Gabriel Marest, speaking about winters in Hudson's Bay wrote: 'this long winter, although always cold, isn't always the same. There are some beautiful days. What I especially like is that there is never any rain, and that after periods of snow and powder (that is how one calls the fine snow that works its way in everywhere), the air is clean and clear.'" —J.-B. Proulx

No doubt they all must have perished, because we never heard anything of them since.

Toussaint said, "They were lucky. They are better off than we are. The Good Lord took them from this world; it would be a good thing if he would do the same for us."

"You mustn't talk like that," said the Captain. "God knows what we must do; if he punished us with this shipwreck, let's use our resignation to appease his anger. Let his will be done!"

"But what will become of us here? Can we last the winter on this rock?"

"What's the use of falling apart? Pulling our hair out won't make it any better. Let's take heart and trust ourselves to providence."

WINTER ON
A ROCKY REEF

We spent the winter on the vessel. Ice formed around the outer sides of the boat attaching it firmly to the rock; it became as hard and as solid as a deck. The water that had filled half the vessel had frozen through and through. But it had not yet reached the rooms in the forecastle where we sought shelter from the winds. For nourishment, we had only dry flour, which, I can assure you, wasn't very appetizing! For water, only the snow that fell, though we had no means of melting it. It was impossible to light a fire: a tinderbox, flint, matches—we had none. We spent most of our days and nights in our beds under the covers. We only went out on deck from time to time in order to exercise, to take away the numbness and restore circulation. On three sides, the ocean spread out like an immense desert; on the north, the shores of Labrador stretched out in a long, blue line. Three times during this sad winter, severe storms struck with fury, each time further cracking the vessel's already greatly damaged framework and threatening to carry it off the rock and the small island of ice that had formed around it.

At first we were somber and taciturn; then, little by little we grew accustomed to the thought of our sorry end. We jabbered about it under our covers even to the point of laughter. Is there nothing man cannot become accustomed to?

In January, Asselin died of feebleness and the cold. Not long after, Sansterre followed him.

We said to ourselves, "Very soon it will be our turn."

The two corpses lay frozen in their beds. Their presence was a constant reminder to us to prepare for our trip to eternity. By the end of March, we were so weak that we could no longer go out on deck where the wind pierced us and knocked us over. All we could do now was to drag ourselves over to our daily ration of a quarter liter of flour; then we would bury ourselves under the bed covers to maintain and conserve what little amount of body heat we had left. We had resigned ourselves to die; it would be a relief.

The captain was leaving behind a wife and children, the thought of which was torture to his soul. But for my brother and me, orphans without friends or relatives, life didn't have the same attraction. Any moment now would be our last.

Around the eighth of April, three young men boarded our vessel, climbed onto the deck, and descended into our cabin. They didn't expect to find anyone alive on what they believed to be an abandoned ship. When they saw us, they recoiled in horror thinking they were coming face to face with ghosts. We were as pale as sheets, as gaunt as skeletons, our haggard eyes staring in their direction. It was a couple of minutes before they could speak.

"What happened to you here?" one of them asked.

Our Captain explained about the shipwreck and finished by saying, "Are you going to bring help for us?"

The young men were very moved, tears welled up in their eyes.

"It is impossible to take you with us at this time," they said. "You are too feeble and there is too much bad ice. We will return to our ship and come back with help. In the meantime, take courage!"

They were three Englishmen from Newfoundland who were hunting seal.[23] We sadly watched them move off, running on the floating islands of ice, leaping from one ice-floe to the next with the aid of their long iron poles, or gaffs. With tears in our eyes we said to each other, "Will they come back? No! They will forget

us. This is certainly the end for us."

Nevertheless, this visit raised our hopes; it doesn't take much to rekindle in the human heart the will to live. We clung to the promise of these three strangers like shipwrecked men to a piece of

23. By the late eighteenth century, sealing became an important industry in Newfoundland and seal was its largest export after cod. In the so-called "Golden Age of Sealing," 1818 to 1862, more than half a million seals (mainly harp seals) were caught annually. Men with gaffs would descend from schooners to go out on foot onto the treacherous ice floes to hunt the seals; it was an extremely hazardous occupation. Today, over a quarter of a million harp seals are slaughtered annually.

flotsam. The sun had become warmer, and each day, for better or worse, we dragged ourselves out on deck and passed the hours scanning the horizon.

Fifteen days went by slowly and grimly without anyone coming. We beseeched God; the captain fell on his knees and raised his hands to the sky. "Lord," he said, "we are moaning and crying in this valley of tears. Have pity on us. Good, sweet, pious Virgin Mary, give us the strength to endure."

We wept bitterly. The prayer ended, Toussaint climbed on deck while the captain and I remained in our cabins depressed and discouraged. All of a sudden, Toussaint let out what seemed to be a real cry of despair that made us shudder.

"Captain," he shouted, "don't be afraid, it's our good friends who are returning!"

We could no longer feel any joy and for a long time we were unable to speak or move. The English fishermen carried us aboard their boat like babes in their arms. They fed us bouillon, and little by little we regained our strength, so much so, that by the end of two weeks, gaffs in hand, we helped them chase after seals.

A month later, they set us ashore in St. John's, Newfoundland where an English steamer transported us to Bordeaux. From Bordeaux to St. Malo was only a hop. Imagine the joy and surprise of our St. Malo friends. They had long ago pictured us at the bottom of the sea as food for the fish; and here we arrived without warning like spirits from beyond the grave.

# 4

## *Gaining My Freedom*

MY FIRST
DESERTION

*A* sailor never gets well acquainted with leisure, for in no time we departed on a frigate commissioned to protect French rights along the coasts of Newfoundland. In addition to the crew, the ship carried about fifty soldiers commanded by a superior officer, although the command of the vessel always rested with Captain Cottin. The soldiers lent us a hand only during difficult maneuvers; otherwise, they practiced military exercises and relaxed in the sun. At the end of June, we found ourselves once more in the port of St. John.

In port I said to my brother, "Should we desert? What a sad life we are leading. It's virtual slavery: no relatives, no friends, no sleep on nights of watch, work in all kinds of weather, beatings, shipwrecks, death awaiting us at every turn. We should go to Canada

**Frigate** (Fr. *Frégate*)

Frigates first appeared in the 16th century, as lightly armed, small, fast and maneuverable vessels. By the early 19th century they had grown in size, the largest class of them carrying 60 cannon (30 pounders) on a single deck, and a crew of 500. Frigates served both as warships and as merchant sailing vessels where cannon were necessary for defending cargo and crew against piracy. They were also the preferred vessels of the famous corsairs Robert Surcouf and René Duguay-Trouin (see boxed text, p.28-9). Frigates evolved into the modern day cruiser.

and try to find our parents. Then on land, we will be men, the same as others."

"Okay!" said my brother, "Let's desert!"

We left at night. We had already passed through the town's streets and had traveled quite a distance into the countryside when three *habitants*[24] went to alert the police that two sailors from the frigate were running away. That night we were brought back under arms to the vessel and thrown into the brig where we spent six

---

24. "In Canada, *habitant* means farmer. In the early days of the colony, the population was divided into two distinct parts, the winterers [*hivernants*] who remained in Quebec only as long as their business required, and the *habitants* who chose to reside in the countryside. The latter worked mostly in cultivating the land, and from there the word became synonymous with farmer." —J.-B. Proulx

From *Webster's New World College Dictionary*, 4th Edition: " habitant: 2. a farmer in Louisiana or Canada of French descent."

days on water and black biscuits. Then we were court-martialed and sentenced: twelve lashes for my brother and twenty for me. I was given the greater punishment because I was the instigator of the desertion.

The day after the trial, towards one in the afternoon, a sergeant opened the door of the brig and solemnly intoned, "Prisoners, come this way to receive your lashes."

A cold shiver ran through us. They led us to the foot of the great mast, made us take off our shirts, put our feet into irons and, with our arms outstretched, fastened our hands to two rings fixed above our heads. The soldiers stood in a double line. Each blow resounded loudly in the midst of silence. I twisted like a worm and couldn't prevent myself from groaning pitifully. At the eighteenth stroke, my endurance gave out and I lost consciousness. The doctor declared that I could take no more. My brother received his twelve lashes without making a sound. I was in bed for six weeks almost without the strength to move. The salve that the doctor put on my sores made me suffer almost as much as the whip. When I had sufficiently recovered, I received my two remaining lashes. Thus I paid my debt down to the last *obole.**

MY SECOND
DESERTION

At the end of July 1870, after having brought a supply of coal to Pictou, our ship reached the north coast of Newfoundland, there to complete its mission. We had barely arrived at our destination

* Farthing or quarter of a cent

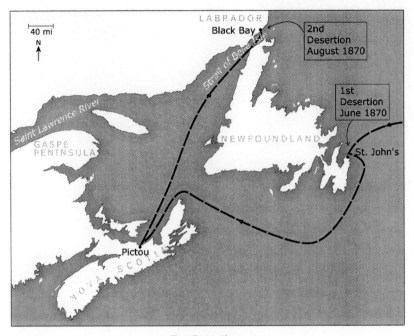

Two Desertions

when, on the first of August, the captain called all hands on deck and in a voice charged with emotion told us, "I have important news to give you. War has been declared between France and Prussia![25] I have just received a telegram calling us into the honors and hazards of service. We leave on the sixth of this month."

We applauded these words, each of us burning with patriotic zeal to pit ourselves against the Prussians.

25. In the Franco-Prussian War of 1870-71, Prussian Chancellor Bismarck manipulated France into declaring war on Prussia. After Germany slaughtered France's newly recruited armies and blockaded Paris, the war ended with France's defeat and brought about the Paris Commune of 1871 wherein Parisians rebelled against the French government—the new Third Republic which replaced the recently overthrown Second Empire under Napoleon III—and set up an autonomous local government, which the state brutally crushed a few months later.

Black Bay, 1998

While passing by Black Bay[26] on the coast of Labrador, the captain said to us, "Go ashore, I am giving all of you a day of rest and relaxation."

In no time, the six shallops were in the water and we (sailors, soldiers, sergeants, and captains) dashed to jump into them. Ashore, we did rifle practice, ran along the beach, enjoyed a good meal in the fresh air, and stretched out on the grass. It was splendid.

The drill sergeant who had led our exercises came over to me and proposed desertion once again.

I told him, "It's too hard for me even to start out since I still haven't recovered from my wounds. In my present condition if we were recaptured, I don't think I could survive another whipping."

26. "Black Bay is located in the Strait of Belle-Isle, on the coast of Labrador, almost directly across from the northernmost point of Newfoundland." —J.-B. Proulx

The location of Black Bay is as little known to outsiders today as it was in Proulx's day. It is not to be found on most current maps and there are no roads going into Black Bay; the nearest road terminates in the adjacent community of Red Bay.

"It's not a matter of whipping," he replied. "To put it simply, we are gambling with our lives. This is wartime. Any deserter who gets arrested gets shot. So make up your mind."

"All right," I told him. "Sound out the other men; if they are ready to go, I'll follow you."

The five others who made up our little band swore they were ready for anything. Seizing a favorable moment, we slipped away from camp around four in the afternoon. We followed a creek from Black Bay to the end of an outflow bordered by firs. To the southwest on our left, rose a high mountain; on our right, spread out flat land dotted with small pine trees and bounded by a range of hills about a half a mile away. Like wolves, we went, one after the other, silently, stealthily, and always on the lookout. My heart was beating wildly.

After a half-hour's march, the sergeant said, "Follow me, my brave comrades, to the top of this rock."

We climbed and climbed each trying to outdo the other. The summit was covered with snow.

"Now we must throw off our tracks all those who attempt to follow us," said our leader. "Take off your boots and put them on your feet backwards."

No sooner said than done. A quarter of an hour later we had gone across the ledge of snow and were descending the opposite side of the mountain.

"Put your boots back on properly," said the sergeant. "Here we must separate. Together we run the risk of dying of hunger. Also, when separated, if one group is caught, the others at least will have a chance of escaping."

Tears came to our eyes; the more we looked at each other, the more the tears ran. Finally we shook hands and said our farewells for life. Wishing the best for each other, we divided into three bands, each going off in a different direction: one toward the southwest, one toward the north, and the last toward the northeast. "May God protect you! May you get back to your country safely! May you be reunited with your families!"

My companion was my brother Toussaint Marin. We marched on until nightfall. At about six o'clock, Toussaint said, "If we could just make it to this second mountain, we could build a shelter there for the night."

With the grace of God and after much weariness, we made it. Choosing a cavity in a rock, we enclosed it with a wall made of stones of different shapes and sizes. This gave us shelter from animals and bad weather. What's more, if we were pursued, no one would think that any humans were behind these stones piled up without symmetry; our crude wall appeared to be a heap of stones that nature had thrown together haphazardly.

We lay down without eating. About nine o'clock we began to hear the booms of cannon fired from the vessel. From time to time, we could see the ominous flashes of exploding bombs. The noise rumbled in and around the mountains like thunder and made the ground tremble. During the next two days, the artillery kept firing hourly. Undoubtedly, they wanted to give us a signal for retracing our steps in case we were accidentally lost; but more likely, they had already sent out pursuers and the sounds indicated where to return once they had captured the deserters.

That night we couldn't stop shaking, but we were so tired we managed to sleep. I kept watch until midnight while Toussaint slept; he spelled me off until daybreak.

THE COAST OF

LABRADOR

We spent five days in this spot never daring to go farther for fear of running into some party of soldiers deployed to find us. From our observation point, we could see the ocean about four miles away and a column of smoke rising from where the ship must have laid at anchor; the crest of a rock blocked our view of the ship and its masts. The scrubby trees in the area were so short that a standing man would be a full head taller than the treetops. We dragged ourselves around flat on our stomachs in order to gather roots and wild atacas and pembinas.[27] We had a rifle, powder and shot, but no game passed by our threshold. At night we could hear wolves all around us and fear kept us from leaving. How could we have beaten them off in the darkness? To tell the truth, we were not doing too well.

On the sixth day, I said to Toussaint, "The frigate must have left by now, let's go farther, maybe we will find some kind of sustenance."

"We had better not go near the shore yet; they may still be prowling around there for us, having silenced the cannon in order to lull us into a trap. Or maybe they commissioned some fishermen to capture us, and the Jerseyans would sell us out in an instant for a slab of bacon."

This is the plan we adopted: we would follow the Labrador coast, always keeping to the interior, until we reached a Canadian settlement, like Natashquan or Mingan,* remote enough to have

---

*See map p. 72.

27. "Ataca and pembina are Algonquian names of wild fruits, which are red when ripe; the first is as big as a cherry, the second is a little smaller."
—J.-B. Proulx

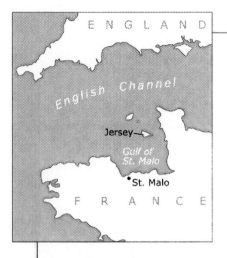

**Jerseyans**

With the Norman Conquest of 1066, the French island of Jersey became part of the British Isles. Over the centuries Jerseyans elected to remain with Great Britain rather than France, though French, or a dialect called Jerrias, remained their main language and the island was much closer to France.

In the 1600s many Jerseyans sailed to Newfoundland to fish for cod. After 1764, when the war between Great Britain and France ended and France lost all claims to Canada, many Jersey fishermen moved to Nova Scotia, especially around Cheticamp, that had formerly belonged to the Acadians before the British expelled them in 1755 (see boxed text p. 68). A Jerseyan Charles Robin came to Nova Scotia in 1764 to start a branch of his family's fishing business that in the next century became the largest fishing company of Canada. Robin brought over many Jerseyans and later employed returning Acadians. Does this history account for Toussaint's apparent distrust of Jerseyans?

missed the news of our desertion. From there, we would get passage on a boat for Quebec. Then we would travel around Canada searching for our parents. This last thought made us smile: the pleasure of finding a mother and father, brothers and sisters. Finally, we too would have a home to relax in and be with friends.

"But," Toussaint would object, "in a country this big, where will we find our family? It will be like looking for a needle in a haystack."

"Our kidnapping must have made some noise back then," I replied. "By announcing that we are lost children, public opinion will surely lead us to the parish where we should look."

"Perhaps we will start our search so far from our birthplace that no one there will have heard about our misfortune."

"We will travel all around Canada; then we will use the newspapers."

"And will our parents recognize us after so many years? We were so young when we were kidnapped from their tender care."

"Who knows? There may still be a family resemblance. Besides, our age will correspond to the time of our kidnapping. After all this, let's have faith in providence. Our most pressing need is to get out of here."

"Yes, yes," said he raising his eyes heavenward, "let us put our faith in the hands of providence which has never abandoned us, and may it keep us safe for our old parents."

With these and similar words we kept up our courage and dodged the demons of hunger. We trekked all day long, dragging our feet over moss and stone, climbing, descending, always with nothing solid to eat but the raspberries and wild fruits that we found along the way. By nightfall, our knees were buckling. We built another shelter on the model of the first one, and there we stretched out full length as if ready to die. Our beds were soft; a thick moss carpeted all the rocks. Everywhere, moss took the place of soil, grass and trees. But if this moss offered a good covering for sleeping, it was a very poor carpet for walking. We often sank into it, like into a sponge, up to our knees.

"I'm hungry," I said to Toussaint.

"Me too," he replied. "Oh, if only God would let us stumble across a piece of bread, how we would eat it with pleasure."

An hour later, two partridges came to rest about twenty paces from our shelter. Toussaint picked up our gun and killed them with a single shot. I ran to get them, and we devoured them instantly without having cooked them. They were so good! It was the first meat we had since leaving the ship.

The next day we were very sick; the raw partridges had not agreed with us. We were forced to remain there for four days, unable to walk, and subsisting on wild fruit. Discouragement worked its way into our hearts. But outwardly, throughout these trying times, I always tried to appear cheerful around my brother.

"It was crazy of us to run away," he would say. "If we had stayed, we wouldn't be in so much trouble."

"If it was madness to leave, let's guard against the further madness of despair. That will be our ruin. Remember what you often said to me, that providence has never abandoned us. And then our parents. . . ?"

The thought of our mother and father always enabled a ray of light to poke through the darkest clouds.

ENCOUNTERING

A BEAR

Having somewhat recovered after four days of rest, we decided, come what may, to continue on our journey. We could barely walk.

Just as Toussaint was saying, "My head is spinning, I can't go any farther," I interrupted him shouting, "Look at this big animal coming at us!"

It was a bear. A large rock was nearby and we raced to it. I jammed the rifle butt into one of its crevices; Toussaint put his foot onto the end of the rifle barrel; I helped him up with my two hands, and he managed to hoist himself to the top of the rock. He held out his arms and pulled me up. We barely had time to grab our rifle. Already the beast had its two front paws on the side of the rock, feasting on us with its glittering eyes, its mouth gaping open, and growling. Breathlessly, we looked at each other, astounded, petrified.

Toussaint took aim and fired; the bullet passed through the bear's jaw and shoulder. It let out a sharp cry as it fell. I took the rifle and fired a second shot through its heart; it was dead. We quickly climbed down, and in no time, we had sliced a hunk of flesh from its rump and ate it bloody and raw. We made a veritable banquet of it; never in our lives had we enjoyed a meal more.

Toussaint said, "If God would continue to send us fresh meat like this, we could very well hope to reach the end our journey."

"Yes," I said, "let's give thanks." Dropping to our knees and doffing our hats, we recited all our prayers in the warm, bright sunshine. It was as though nature rejoiced with us.

## HEADING TOWARDS
## THE OCEAN

We spent two days beside this larder that God put on our path. We were starting to regain our strength, but the bear was beginning to smell.

I said to my companion, "Let's each cut off a slab and go. If you're willing, we'll try to reach the sea; the ship must have left long ago. It would not have delayed its departure any longer for seven men like us. Maybe they didn't commission any of the settlers to arrest us. In any case, given a choice of death, I'd prefer to draw my last breath among humans than among wild beasts. What do you say, brother?"

"Brother, I'm with you," he replied.

We resumed our journey with a firm stride; we hadn't marched with such aplomb since the beginning of our desertion. We talked about the joy of seeing our parents.

But sad thoughts often returned to dash Toussaint's hopes. He would say, "Our mother and father are probably dead and soon we will be, too."

"We must always be hopeful," I replied. "It's been about twenty-five years since we were kidnapped, our parents wouldn't be too old today. In any case, we must still have some brothers and sisters; we will find some member of our family. "

"I wish it, I want it, but I doubt it. Something tells me I will end up leaving my bones in this inhospitable land." This was his daily refrain.

We had been walking for five long weeks without reaching the ocean. The sky was usually dark and cloudy, the sun rarely showing its face. We had obviously gone off course. From time to time we killed a partridge or some other kind of bird, equally meaty. But for the last fifteen days we hadn't had any meat at all. Our strength had really given out.

Toussaint said, "We must make camp here and rest for a few days, I can't drag myself any farther."

We found ourselves at the edge of a lake about ten miles long by five miles wide. On one side was flatland[28] about three miles wide and bordered by a high mountain.

Toussaint said, "Let's sleep at the foot of this mountain."

For overnight, we preferred high places to flat ground. There we could more easily find caves, excavations, or stones to build a shelter. Usually we would come upon a stream running down from the mountain on the edge of which we would build our camp.

In the middle of the field, Toussaint, exhausted, threw himself on the ground saying, "I am dying of hunger."

We hadn't found any fruit since that morning. I got to my knees, took off my hat and recited the prayer that had comforted us so often.

I had hardly finished this prayer when I walked a few steps and found an abundance of atacas. I called my brother over; he gobbled down the fruit with both hands. After we had eaten our fill, we said, "Let's give thanks to the Virgin," which we did with all our hearts.

A quarter of an hour later we were at the foot of the mountain building our shelter for the night. We were not able to find water in the surrounding area. The work proceeded slowly; our legs were like rubber, our arms worn out. We kept sinking painfully into the thick bed of dried up moss that covered the ground. Toussaint, es-

---

28. flatland (*flatte*): "The Canadians have undoubtedly taken this word from the English 'flat,' *plat*, however it is more French than you think. The *Académie* preserved '*flatir*,' to hammer the discs [*flans*] of coins on the anvil, that is to say to flatten them; and '*flatoir*,' the large hammer used to flatten the discs." —J.-B. Proulx

Proulx was writing about the process of minting coins; the words "*flatir*" and "*flatoir*" are no longer to be found in standard French dictionaries.

pecially, was more often sitting down than standing up; I had never seen him so completely overcome. The night looked menacing, the sky was full of clouds, and my heart filled with dread.

## MY BROTHER'S DEATH

Two hours after lying down on our moss beds, having slept lightly, I awoke, sat up, and looked at my brother. He was as white as a sheet, moaning, his lips drawn.

"Are you sick" I asked?

"Yes, very sick."

Soon he began to tremble all over, so much so, that his teeth chattered. He was writhing from spasms and choking from cramps; he vomited painfully; his groans were ear splitting. "I'm suffering," he said, "as much as one can suffer. If this keeps up, I will die."

I sat there with my arms crossed, dismayed, mute. I couldn't find a single word to say. My poor brother was rolling around in agony, but I couldn't bring him any relief. And he complained constantly.

He also suffered from thirst. "Louis, Louis," he said in a voice that stabbed my heart, "dear Louis, get me some water, just a drop of water. My throat is parched and my insides are on fire."

It was a good three miles to the lake. The night was very dark and I could hear the wolves howling around our camp.

"My poor brother," I replied, "it pains me so much to see you suffer so, to hear your anguish and not to be able to help you. But you must understand that I can't go outside at this time. The lake is too far, I wouldn't be able to find my way in the dark, and I couldn't go fifty feet before the wolves would finish me off. If you can just wait until daylight, I will gladly get you water!"

"Will it be long 'til morning?" he asked.

"An hour and a half or two at most." How slowly the time passed.

"I am suffering, Louis, it's so painful! I am asking God to let me die. I can't take it any longer. Yes, death will be welcome!"

Before such terrible suffering, I felt my heart grow heavy. I kept silent, not finding any words of consolation equal to his suffering.

As dawn was breaking, I said to Toussaint, "Are you still thirsty?"

"Yes, yes, very thirsty."

"Okay, I'll find you some water, but don't get discouraged if I take a while. As you know the lake is a long way off."

With the carbine on my shoulder, I started out; I had no other container for water but the barrel of my gun. My legs were so weak that I stumbled with nearly every step. I felt lightheaded and the trees around me seemed to dance before my eyes. About three hundred yards from the lake, I could go no farther and sat down on a large flat rock.

"Blessed Virgin," I cried, "help me. Give me something to eat. If not, I won't be able to go back up the hill; I will die here while my brother dies back there."

Somehow, painfully and miserably, I reached the lake. Just as I was bending down to fill the barrel of my carbine, I heard a rustling noise in the rushes, which made my blood run cold. I looked, and to my surprise, I saw that a large trout had gotten itself stranded in the mud. Faster than you can count to three, I leapt on top of it and threw it onto the bank. Then, with the fish in one hand and the gun in the other, I started back up the mountain path. Arriving at the same big rock, I sat down again and made a good meal of half the fish. Hope and strength returned. I knelt down on the stone that had served as my dinner table and seat. My head uncovered, facing the lake, I thanked the Virgin for the beautiful present she gave me.

Though trembling with sadness, I now walked with a firmer step. I looked all around wide-eyed with apprehension. I seemed to see my brother's ghost jumping out at me from every bush in this forest of dwarf trees. When I finally arrived at our shelter, shaking all over and blinded by a cold sweat, I asked myself in anguish, "Is he still alive or is he dead?" Before entering, I looked through a hole in the craggy wall and saw Toussaint. It was almost a relief to see him fitfully tossing and turning in his bed.

"Brother," I asked, "how are you now?"

"Very weak," he said.

"Are you thirsty?"

"Yes."

I gave him the end of the carbine. He could no longer sit up by himself.

He drank only a few drops and said, "That's good, that's enough, thanks." He added with a shaky voice, "I'm very hungry."

"If you have some food will you have the strength to eat?" I replied.

"Yes, with all my heart!"

I cut a piece of the fish and gave it to him, and he grasped my hand. He wanted to smile but his drawn features managed only to produce a grimace. I realized that the end was near.

When he had eaten he said, "I feel better. It's funny but it seems that it's not thirst that makes me suffer so, but hunger. If I hadn't eaten I couldn't last the day. I don't feel any more pain. I'll sleep, I can't keep my eyes open."

His glassy, dull eyes stared fixedly at me.

I said to him, "Before going to sleep, let's recommend your soul to God."

"Why do that?" he replied, "You think I'm in a bad way?"

"My dear brother, I'm afraid so," I said.

"No, no, I feel much better."

Then he fell asleep. I knelt by his side, feeling very sad and praying. I thought of Jesus, who in his dying moments said, "My soul is sad unto death."

Half an hour later he woke up with pains in his left side and cramps in every limb. I massaged his body to give him some comfort. He let out heart-rending cries and writhed in pain.

He kept repeating, "I'm going to die, I want to die. I can't bear this suffering.

"Only one thing troubles me and that is leaving you all alone in this wasteland. What will happen to you? If you should get sick, who will take care of you? If you die, who will bury you? You'll be prey to wild animals. At least for me, I have a brother who will see that my body is in the ground."

"My dear brother, banish these sad thoughts," I replied. "Confide in God's mercy, and recite with me once more the prayer we never forget to say each night: 'Most Holy Mary, my Mother and my Queen, I am going to throw myself upon your tender mercy, and, from this moment on, put my body and soul under your special protection for all the days of my life, and for the hour of my death. I am putting into your hands all my hopes and consolations, all my trials and miseries, the whole of my life, so that, through your holy intercession, my deeds and intentions may be put in order according to your Divine Son's will.'"

At about eleven thirty, Toussaint became calmer; his endurance had given out, his face had become pale and livid, his gaze unfocused and wandering. I felt his pulse; it was feeble.

"My dear Louis," he said in a barely audible voice. "Good-bye, I'm dying. If you find our parents tell them how much we suffered far from them, and how much I would have loved to see them again. God willed otherwise, and we shall see each other in heaven. Come near so I can embrace you once more. May God help you in your suffering. Good-bye, my brother. These are the last words I say to you. I feel my heart weakening. Good-bye."

His death throes lasted for about twenty-five minutes. He lay quietly on his bed, only his chest raised and lowered with difficulty. I watched him and cried. Around noontime, he gently passed away. I could barely discern his last breath. I remained seated near him, overcome with grief, my heart constricted with stifled emotion, my eyes dry. I had no more tears.

Outside, as well as inside myself, everything was somber. The sky was overcast and large dark clouds enveloped the mountaintop. Snow fell in fine, hard pellets, the wind whistled through the treetops, and I shivered from the cold and renewed sobbing. A fountain of tears started gushing again over my brother's body.

"I want to die here," I cried. "It's useless to carry my poor bones any farther. I'll never make it out of this forest. We were together all our lives, my dear brother, we will be together again in death."

I spent the afternoon lying down next to his corpse, resolved to make no further efforts to gather wild fruits, just to lie in our refuge until the little bit of life left in me ebbed away.

At dusk, I got on my knees and dug with my hands down through the moss to make a grave about two feet deep where I placed his body. I carried over stones and piled them around the sides with the plan of making a covering as soon as I began to feel my strength failing me for the last time. Then I closed the doorway with a large flat rock thinking, "Farewell light of day, this shelter will be my tomb."

The snow had stopped but the wind's dismal whistling continued. Attracted no doubt by the odor of a dead body, the wolves were howling in chorus and working all around my poorly built shelter to gain an entrance. I took my carbine and fired three or four shots. The noise echoing again and again through the mountains made my hair stand on end. I spent a sleepless night. There was only myself to hold the wake[29] for my brother's body and to pray for his soul, which I did unceasingly.[30] I addressed my words sometimes to Jesus, sometimes to His Blessed Mother. "Open your heart to me, Jesus, because this is my final resting place. I wish my whole life to be there and to make my last breath there. Do not abandon me, Mother of Mercy. Protect me during my days of pilgrimage and guard my soul at the hour of death."

I remained there three days, watching over and crying for my brother who was no more. The will to live is deeply rooted in the

29. "In our rural areas, when a person dies, the body is put on view, and, during the two or three nights before burial, friends and relatives gather in great number around the body and pass the time either in pious reading, in silent meditation, or in saying the rosary." —J.-B. Proulx

30. "*Décesser* [stop, cease], according to Littré, a popular barbarism used instead of *cesser* [cease]. But in their usage of it the people give it much more force than the latter word." —J.-B. Proulx

human heart and I felt it reawaken in me, weak at first, and then grow stronger. I resolved to try to prolong my pitiful existence. Also, after some reflection, I realized that I wasn't permitted to let myself die through inaction. I didn't want to arrive at the Tribunal of Justice with suicide on my conscience. Three or four times a day I went out to gather a meal of atacas and roots. Anyway, grief and weakness had greatly diminished my appetite.

On the fourth day I piled all the stones and rocks I had gathered over my brother's body, and over that I heaped on the wreckage of our shanty to ensure that his remains would find shelter from any attack or desecration by wild animals. I fashioned a wooden cross with my knife and placed it atop his grave mound so that anyone ever passing this way would know a Christian was buried here.

Kneeling, my head uncovered, I prayed a long time for the one I was going to leave. "Lord, give him eternal rest. He has suffered so much in his short life. His joys were few, his pains many. Surely he has done enough penance down here for his sins. *Requiescat in Pace*, rest in peace. My poor brother, my dear friend, my lifelong, inseparable companion, good-bye. I mourn leaving you. As you are no doubt in heaven, listen to me, protect me, and guide me through all the difficulties that I have still to confront in this land of mud and misery."

It was very hard for me to go. My spirit was broken; and I felt as though I were leaving a piece of my heart under this pile of rocks. I walked a few hundred yards and then stopped to return to the mountain. I shed a torrent of tears. These moments have remained sharply etched in my memory all my life. I remembered Toussaint's kindness, his friendship for me, all that we had gone through together, both good and bad.

I started talking to myself, "What will become of me without my brother? No one else has loved me and now I am alone in these woods. Even if I should manage to find myself among people again, I will still be alone. My good friend will never again be at my side to share in my future. Can I ever be happy without him?"

I was very feeble and proceeded slowly looking backwards as much as forwards. What a sad day that was!

## MEETING A <u>MÉTIS</u>

That night I was too tired and dispirited to build a shelter. I lay under the stars in a rocky cranny that I covered with branches. I was restless all night and slept very little, the image of my brother was everywhere I looked.

At daybreak, I resumed my journey. My goal was to reach the sea where I would throw myself at the first fisherman's shack I came across. To be taken prisoner, returned to the ship, given twenty lashes, brought before a firing squad, none of that bothered me. On the contrary, death seemed to me an enviable fate.

I had been walking for a few hours when suddenly I saw in the distance something drawing near. Was it an animal? Was it a man? Was it one of the ship's soldiers in disguise searching for me? I hid behind a large rock, quaking like a leaf. I realized then that I clung to life more than I thought!

Man or beast, it kept advancing until it was but a few a few hundred steps away. I risked a look. It saw me, and cried in rather bad French, *"Toi, pas peur; j'étions un ami."**

This turned out to be a *Métis*, half-Acadian, half-Inuit, who was hunting caribou in the mountains. He was dressed from head

*"You, no fear; I were a friend."

to toe completely in fur: in sealskin boots, sealskin pants, a sealskin jacket, and a sealskin hood. He stepped back in surprise when he saw how gaunt I was; I must have looked like a skeleton.

"Where are you from?" he asked.

I hope God will forgive me for the story I made up—I replied, "I was a sailor on a French ship. The Captain gave us all a day's shore leave. That night they pulled up anchor before I was on board, no doubt believing that all the men had returned. Since then I have been wandering around these rocks lost."

"For how long?"

"For definitely over two months!"

"What did you live on?"

"Begging your pardon, on lots of inedible filth: roots, wild fruit, dead fish crawling with worms, rotting jellyfish.[31] It's amazing how little a person can survive on. My friend, take pity on me and give me something to eat."

"All right, follow me and come to my lodging."

He had built a comfortable shelter out of wood for himself. His furnishings had the luxury of a small sheet-iron stove, with a copper boiler on it. Roasting over the embers was a large piece of caribou. The delicious aroma made my mouth water. I could not help smiling with anticipation; it had been almost three weeks since I had tasted so much as a mouthful of meat. This meal did me a lot of good. I stayed for three days with this good man who treated me like a brother. At night, I slept deeply, free from worry; my health returned. How fortunate it was to find a compassionate soul in my hour of need! May God reward this stranger in the wilderness for saving my life and putting me back on the road to civilization.

31. "From what I could understand [from Cholet], these sea suns [*soleils de mer*] were types of polyps with soft and contractible bodies."—J.-B. Proulx

**Métis and Louis Riel**

Métis are most often the descendants of the *voyageurs* (who were generally French Canadian, see boxed text p. 111) and First Nations women.

The *Métis* Pierre encountered here was "half-Acadian, half-Inuit." Acadians were the French colonists who settled in Nova Scotia, Prince Edward Island (then known as Ile St. Jean) and along the coast from Quebec to Maine. During the war between France and England over control of Canada—the French and Indian War, itself an important segment of the Seven Years War (1756-1763), though it began two years earlier—the English expelled Acadians from their land, forcing many onto ships taking them to ports in France (such as St. Malo), England, and the English colonies to the south. Beginning with the Great Expulsion of 1755, several thousand Acadians were displaced, a third of them dying in the exodus. Many Acadians made their way to southern Louisiana, where they became known as Cajuns. Some fled into northern New Brunswick. After the war, some Acadians eventually returned to Canada mostly to the area around Chaleur Bay, Ristigouche and the Gaspé Peninsula (see map p. 72 and boxed text p. 79).

"Deportation of the Acadians in 1755." *Le Monde illustré*, 23 April 1898. Courtesy of BAnQ.

Louis Riel

In the mid 1800s, *Métis* lived all over Canada and were the majority of settlers in the Red River Settlement.

The *Métis* were involved in two violent struggles with English settlers over land rights. The first was the Red River Rebellion of 1869 under the leadership of Louis Riel. This successfully resulted in the 1870 Manitoba Act that turned Red River Settlement into the province of Manitoba and granted *Métis* demands for separate French Catholic schools for *Métis* children. The second was the North-West Rebellion of 1884-1885. Under pressure from incoming European settlers, the Métis had been moving further west to find secure land. However, the expansion of the Canadian National Railways sped the westward advance of English settlers that again threatened *Métis* settlements around today's Saskatchewan. The *Métis* again called upon Louis Riel, then in exile in the US since the earlier rebellion, to lead their armed struggle. This time the Canadian Mounties completely defeated the *Métis* and Riel was captured, tried for treason, and executed in 1885. Many French Canadians protested his execution. This happened the year before Proulx first met Cholet. Did Proulx and Cholet know of Louis Riel, and sympathize with the plight of the *Métis* as did many French Canadians? It seems likely. Proulx had been a missionary in Manitoba in 1871-74, not long after the Red River Rebellion, and he later got involved in the Manitoba School Crisis of 1896 (see boxed text p. 10).

"The execution of Louis Riel." *Le Monde illustré,* 5 December 1885. Courtesy of BAnQ.

"Do I have far to go to reach the sea?" I asked him

"Twenty miles."

"How can I reach it?"

"From other side of this mountain." He pointed south, south-west.

"Would you do me another favor?" I asked before we parted.

"What?"

"Exchange clothes with me."

"You can't be serious! Your clothes are so much better than mine."

"It's nothing," I said, "It's the only way I can show my thanks."

I insisted. It was a lucky break for me. Who would recognize me in such an outfit? At last he consented. We parted with a handshake; he to hunt and me to find the sea; he dressed as a French

"An Inuit and his kayak."
*Le Monde illustré,* 27 Aug.
1887. Courtesy of BAnQ.

"French sailors in Montreal."
*Le Monde illustré,* 22 Sept.
1894. Courtesy of BAnQ.

sailor and I as an Inuit, in fur clothing that was all of one piece: shoes, pants, jacket and hood. In effect, I was bristling with fur like a bear or a wolf. I looked at my reflection in the glassy surface of the lake and couldn't stifle a burst of laughter—I looked so comical.

I was in good shape, a hunk of caribou on my shoulders, my courage restored.

"I can live among men again and perhaps find my parents. In any case, I can surely reach my birthplace and make some friends there, a pleasure I have never savored and which must be so sweet."

This train of thought made it easy to climb the mountains and to bear wearing the fur clothing that was both too hot and was crawling with lice. Although I was drenched in sweat, high hopes buoyed me up. Already I breathed in the sea air, and its saltiness transported me like a foretaste of liberty. In short, if the memory of my brother hadn't pursued me everywhere, casting its shadow over my every thought, I would have been almost happy. Like a mirage in the indeterminate distance, a vision of my homeland appeared.

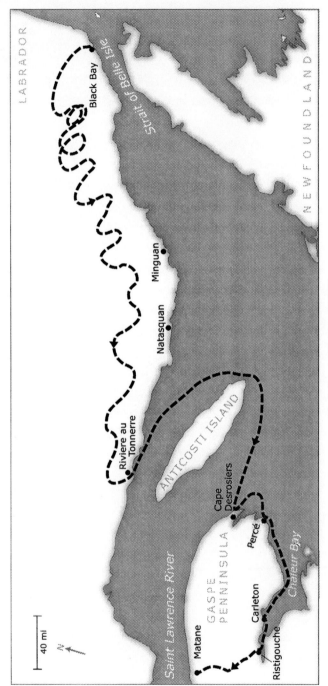

Black Bay to Matane (1870)

5

## *Reaching My Homeland*

*I* walked for two days. I spent the first night in a rocky alcove. Late the second evening, under cover of darkness, I arrived in Rivière-au-Tonnerre, a tiny fishing station consisting of three houses. I hid a short distance away, ever fearful of official or unofficial agents from the frigate. It was a Saturday in mid-October. Near a buoy, about four hundred feet from shore, a sailboat was rocking at anchor. To secure my safety, I made up my mind to steal it. I have often heard it said that in cases of dire need, all property is communal. Was I really in such desperate straits? All I can say is that God who sounds the depth of hearts saw in that moment my good faith and sincere intentions.

I warily jumped into a small rowboat that had been pulled up on the beach. Not wishing to steal anything needlessly, I took care to tie it to the buoy. On the sailboat, I found two large sails folded under the seats. They were absolutely necessary for my getaway. I felt that providence must have been on my side and wished me well. This is why I wasn't afraid to launch the boat out into open sea. Also, in the compartment at the stern lay a candle of tallow, which served as my dinner by midday the following day—when one is very hungry, the palate doesn't dare complain too much.

The good Virgin provided a strong tailwind; I set the two sails, come what may, in the direction of where I thought Anticosti Island lay. The temperature was mild, my stomach empty, and my heart full of hope as the boat flew over the crests of the waves. When daylight appeared, I lowered the sails for fear of being seen from shore and pursued. At noon, without fear, I hoisted the sails high. I had covered enough ground that the curve of the sea hid me from view even with the aid of the most powerful spyglass.

Towards two o'clock, the coast of Anticosti Island began to rise out of the water. My heart hammered in my chest—I hadn't gone astray after all. I pointed the prow toward the lighthouse on the northeastern end of the island. In the gathering darkness, I reached the shore. A Canadian* lived there with his family and operated the lighthouse. They treated me very well, giving me food and lodging for the night as well as a loaf of bread for my voyage the next day. I thought to myself, "How generous the Canadians are; as soon as I get myself among them my troubles will be over."

*"Canadian" means French Canadian

ANTICOSTI

TO GASPÉ

I spent the entire day, night, and part of the next day, tossed about in heavy seas. I could see Cape Desrosier in the distance but I could hardly get any closer because of the strong offshore wind. It had turned freezing cold. Numb, cramped, and frozen, I crouched in the bottom of the boat with one hand on the tiller. I consoled myself by eating the white bread; I was unaccustomed to such flavor and freshness. In Labrador, I had almost starved to death; on my old ship, our only treat was a dark, hard biscuit that had to be soaked in order to soften it before chewing.

Nighttime found me at the entrance to Gaspé Bay. I slept on the bottom of the boat, wrapped up in a sail. At daybreak, I entered the harbor and went to knock on the door of Mr. George Bouthillier, who was a Member of Parliament. An old lady opened the door and upon seeing me in my fur costume let out a frightful cry.

"There's nothing to be afraid of Madam," I said. "I'm a poor unfortunate soul without a penny to his name. For the love of God, would you give me something to eat?"

Mr. Bouthillier appeared and told her to set the table for me. He asked me where I came from, where was I going, what was I looking for. I answered him evasively for fear of being recognized since our ship had come so often into the port of Gaspé.

When the meal was finished, I thanked them, bid them farewell, and continued my sail to Percé.

PERCÉ

The wind was favorable. By six o'clock that night, my boat was gently swaying between a large cliff above which seagulls were continually wheeling about and the small village of Percé, nestled at the foot of a hill.

I called at a boarding house run by an old, white-bearded Jerseyan called Degrouchie.

On viewing me through the door's windowpanes, his three grown daughters cried out, "Papa, don't give this dirty savage any lodging here."

He shouted at me in a surly voice, "You can't sleep here, get on your way!"

I answered him calmly in good French,[32] "My friend, you don't need to get angry, I'm asking for lodging not out of love for me, but rather for the love of God."

As I reached the water's edge, the man called out, "Wait, stranger, are you French or Jerseyan?"

"They say I'm Canadian."

"From what part of Canada?"

"I would have a hard time telling you that. I was stolen when I was just a small child and now I am trying to return to my homeland to find my parents. But goodnight, Sir, it's getting late, and I have to hurry to find lodgings."

"Come back," he said, "and spend the night here."

When he had heard my adventures, big tears rolled down his cheeks, and he reproached himself for having at first refused me

32. Canadian French is distinct in accent and speech from European French. Pierre was educated in St. Malo, France and could speak a "good" French with a noticeable accent from France.

shelter, adding, "It's also the fault of these creatures[33] who are afraid of everything."

"I can't blame them," I said. "Face to face with a stranger as bizarrely dressed, dirty, blackened, and covered with grease, as I am now, maybe I would have acted the same way."

The next morning after breakfast, we parted great friends.

CARLETON

I followed the counties' shoreline from Gaspé to Bonaventure. My strategy was to push on to the bottom of Chaleur Bay, and from there to reach Quebec, where I hoped to get information about my parents. The wind continued to be good, and I was able to sail six or seven knots an hour.

I made a stop at Carleton, at the home of a tanner named Cauchon. The woman of the house took one look at me and fell into a dead faint. Her little girl started yelling at the top of her voice, "Daddy, Daddy, come quick and see this scary man!"

The tanner came running. He knocked me down, kicked me in the legs three or four times, and beat me with a stick. I protested to no avail that I was the most innocent of men; he would not listen. As if he were deaf, he continued hitting me, swearing, cursing, and raging. I managed to get up; limping and hobbling, my body bruised and aching, I reached my boat.

Good-bye Carleton, I will never forget you or your Cauchon.[*]

*In French, "Cauchon" makes a pun with the word "*cochon*" meaning pig.

33. "In Canada, the word creature doesn't in itself contain any bad connotation, and is often used for a girl or a woman." —J.-B. Proulx

RISTIGOUCHE

It was midnight when my boat under full sail entered the silent, deserted port of Ristigouche. The village was built high above the river of the same name. Waiting for dawn, I slept under the boat's seats. When I awoke, I noticed a <u>Micmac</u> man standing on the shore.

"Friend," he said, "where are you from?

"From Labrador."

" You must be telling the truth because you are dressed like the people from there."

"How would you like to buy my boat?" I asked him.

"How much do you want for it?"

"Twenty-five dollars."

"That seems a fair price, I'm coming back, wait a quarter of an hour."

I waited all day and all night, but he never returned. I was sorry I had asked such a high price and discouraged him. Twice that day I went to houses about a mile away where good-hearted Canadian hospitality provided me with food and water.

The next day at dawn, a Jerseyan appeared. Did the Micmac man send him? The Jerseyan didn't say.

"Is that boat for sale?" he asked me.

"Yes."

"How much?"

"Twenty dollars."

"No, that's too much, I'll give you sixteen."

"Very well," I replied, "take it."

While receiving the money, I found out about the road to Matane.

1998 Postcard from Fort Listiquig in Lestuguj Mi'kmaq Nation, then also a tourist hotel.

## Micmac (Mi'kmaq) Nation

"Mi'kmaq" comes from a word meaning "allies" or "my friends". Pierre's encounter with the Micmac man in Ristigouche is his first where he experienced no initial fright or prejudice against his appearance as an Inuit or Métis.

The Micmac Nation was the major tribe of the Canadian Maritimes, particularly Nova Scotia and New Brunswick. They were probably the first New World people to encounter the Europeans, perhaps the Vikings as early as the 11th century and later the first Basque fishermen who arrived before Columbus on Newfoundland's coasts. By the 16th century they routinely traded with the French arrivals, converted to Catholicism, and intermarried with French settlers, the Acadians. But contact with the Europeans brought diseases like smallpox that decimated their population from perhaps 20,000 in the 16th century to less than 2,000 by the early 19th century.

The Micmac nation aided the French in the war with England (the French and Indian War) and sheltered many Acadians during their great deportation from 1755 to 1763, like those who fled north to Ristigouche and environs (see boxed text p. 68).

In 1760 at the mouth of the Ristigouche River, France lost a decisive naval battle to win back Quebec from the English and subsequently gave up all claims to Canada with the Treaty of Paris in 1763.

Today there are about 25,000 Micmac people many of whom live in the several Micmac Reserves in the Maritimes, one of which is in Ristigouche (Lestuguj Mi'kmaq Nation).

The Jerseyan said, "Take this road for about three miles; at the last house just before entering the forest, ask again for directions."

I left on foot, my rifle on my shoulder, feeling jaunty and carefree. For the first time in my life, I really felt free; I was beyond the frigate's reach, and what's more, I never had so much money in my pocket.

My plan now was to reach the banks of the St. Lawrence River, to follow it to Quebec, and from there to search for my parents in earnest.

"My poor brother," I thought, "if only you could have followed me here, how happy we could have been together, now that we are close to reaching the end of our journey. But God willed otherwise! Besides, right now, you might prefer your fate to mine."

## THE ROAD TO
## MATANE

People had told me that the portage, or overland distance, from Ristigouche to Matane was a good ninety miles. With the exception of two small inns, one a few miles from Ristigouche and the other nine or ten miles from Matane, you would not see another house along the entire route. The road ran through swamps, hills and valleys. It was far from beautiful; in reality, it was only an infrequently used trail where wagons would get stuck in its ruts.[34]

From time to time, I passed by cabins (*campes*)[35] built, no doubt, by the workers who had opened this route. They were constructed

34. "This agrees perfectly with the information (in answer to my question) that M. N. Levesque, pastor of Matane gave me: 'There is not really any proper road which goes from Ristigouche to Matane. There are only the traces of an old wagon trail, which is practically never used.'" —J.-B. Proulx

35. "This is the name that the *voyageurs* [see boxed text p. 111-112] and men at work sites give to the lodgings they construct for camping." —J.-B. Proulx

"A forest workers' camp." *Le Monde illustré,* 15 April 1893. Courtesy of BAnQ.

out of logs dovetailed together with a covering of spruce bark; at the back of these rustic dwellings stood rough, stone chimneys. These were the only hostels a traveler could find along this route. At the same time, they served as stables for beasts of burden. I slept in these cabins for three nights, happy nevertheless to have them in order to take cover in inclement weather and to find shelter from wolves. This rich and plentiful forest was like a terrestrial paradise compared to the rocky, barren terrain of Labrador. The walk was good and firm; I had bought food before starting out, so I was no longer consumed with hunger. Three times I encountered wagons; these occasional travelers seemed friendly. I asked them if I was on the right road for Matane and about the distance remaining. Their answers renewed my energy and hope.

However, after so much walking, my feet were bleeding quite badly by the fourth night. Hobbling, I arrived at the hotel, which stood alone in the woods like an advance guard of civilization. It was eight o'clock. I requested lodging.

"Impossible," the innkeeper replied, "there is sickness in the house."

No doubt my costume and appearance made him afraid of me. "How far is it to the next neighbor?" I asked.

"Nine miles."

"You can plainly see," I told him, "that I can't go any farther. My bloody feet refuse to take me. Please take pity on me."

He did not reply, so I sat on a bench near the door, thinking to myself, "This man is English, I can tell by his speech. If only I could get myself to the Canadians my suffering would be over; there I would be welcomed with open arms!"

An illusion! I later discovered for myself that there could be some hard-hearted Canadians, as well as some tenderhearted English; it's a mixed bag.[36] Meanwhile, a stranger arrived by wagon. The master of the house spoke softly in his ear.

"Would you like to come with me?" asked the traveler. "I live fifteen miles from here, a little above Matane."

"With pleasure, Sir; it won't take me out of my way to Quebec."

The ride was agreeable; we talked of one thing and another, and the time passed quickly. But I didn't reveal my life's story to him. It was past midnight, when we reached his home.

THE NIGHT
VISITOR

This man, whose name I've forgotten, invited me to sleep in his house.

"Thank you," I replied, "you've been far too good to me as it is, and I don't want to cause you any trouble. I must warn you that my furry outfit is crawling with lice, and the love of God keeps

36. The long history of rivalry between the French and the English over control of Canada, colonists' struggles over land and political power, together with differences in language, culture, and religion, rendered relations between French and English speaking Canadians thorny. Proulx and Cholet apparently recommended all Canadians to look beyond their inherited prejudices and to judge individuals by their actions in the present.

me from leaving the seeds of this satanic brood in your house. With your permission, I shall spend the rest of the night in your hayloft."

He came up to show me a place and brought me a couple of blankets. I made a hollow in the hay and fell asleep, warm and comfortable.

Two hours later, I was awakened by a noise. A man was cautiously entering the barn. He was carrying several bags under his arms, holding a candle in one hand, and a bucket in the other. I thought that he must be a hired hand coming to prepare a load of grain for the next day. He placed the candle on the floor, and started to fill the bags from a large pile of wheat that had accumulated at the bottom of a chute.

Five were already filled when he began talking to himself, "If I had known, I would have brought my son along, he could have helped me."

"I'll be glad to help you, Mister," I said.

I had hardly spoken the words when he looked around in terror and without any further hesitation, bolted out the door like a streak of lightening. I knew then that he was a thief.

I went over to put out the candle and then lay back down again; but I was much too excited to sleep. I made my way to the house and rapped on the door, but no one answered. I sat on the doorstep for what seemed like an hour. The cold was getting to me; I decided to knock again.

The master got up angrily. "If you don't stop this, fella, I'll get my whip, and then we'll see."

"Excuse me, Sir," I replied, "I've come to see if it was you who came tonight to measure out the wheat in the chute."

"Measure out the wheat!" He was dumbfounded. He followed

me to the barn. We found five bags full of wheat and five others empty. On each bag was written the name of our visitor.

"Thanks," he said, "you have done me a great service. This man has been stealing from me for a long time. I've had my doubts but now I have the proof. This time he'll pay for it, all of it."

After breakfast I wanted to leave.

"Not yet," said the master, "stay here with us until your feet are completely healed. Here, take these clothes and go change in the barn."

He had given me a complete set of clothes made out of flannel and the cloth of the region, not new, but still quite good. I bathed and deloused myself as best as I could, and felt my body relax. The lice, which I had acquired in my exchange with the Inuit, had bitten into me so badly that I still carry scars from them to this day.

I stayed about ten days with this good family. I told them who I was. They wanted to hire me and made me very generous offers.

"No," I told them, "now that providence has brought me to my homeland, I want to search for my parents. For me, this is a sacred obligation, a son's duty. My father and mother must have shed many tears over my kidnapping. If they are still living, I will console them in their old age. Good-bye, I'm going and I'll not stop until my search is crowned with success."

# 6

## *My Long Search*

*I* went back up the coast of the St. Lawrence River—generally on foot, sometimes by wagon—as far as St.-Denis, passing by Métis, Ste.-Flavie, Ste.-Luce, Rimouski, Bic, St.-Fabien, St.-Simon, Trois-Pistoles, Cacouna, Rivière-du-Loup, Kamouraska, St.-Paschal. I stopped at each church along the way to put my journey under the protection of the local patron saint, and to ask him for strength and courage. I felt at peace at the foot of the altar, it being the only place on land where I felt somewhat at home. The people of Lower Quebec were very charitable; I was able to save some of my money for future emergencies. For the love of God, I received food and shelter everywhere.

In mid-November, I arrived in St. Denis. It was snowing and the roads were becoming difficult to travel. I decided to take the

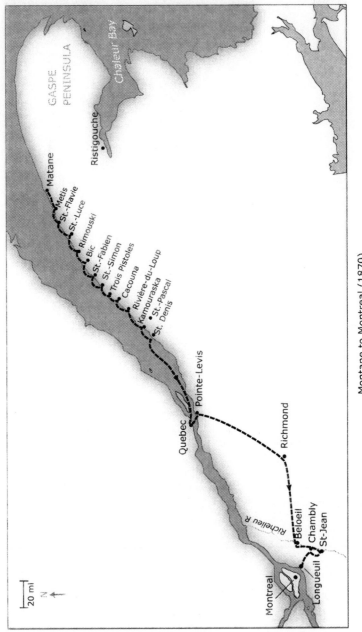

Montane to Montreal (1870)

boat to Quebec City. Every day on that trip, I asked if there were any families by the name of Marin. Nobody knew of any.

In Quebec, I began a more diligent search. Near the market-place of Lower Town, I found lodging at a widow's where many retired river pilots resided. She told me, "Go see the priests in Upper Town. That's where you stand the best chance of getting reliable information."

One of the priests said, that as far as he knew, there were no Marins in Quebec. But he had heard, he didn't know how, that a man by that name lived in Richmond on the road to Montreal, and that he had lost a child, but only one, not three.

"Come with me," he said, "and we will place a notice of your misfortune in the newspaper."

And the next day, I believe it appeared in the Quebec paper as follows:

> Two young brothers, Louis and Toussaint Marin, along with their cousin, Pierre, aged five, four, and six years old, respectively, were kidnapped in 1845. One of the two brothers has been searching for his parents. If anyone has heard anything about a Marin family whose children were lost, would he please give this information to the journal's office?

This notice cost me a dollar. Any responses would be sent im-mediately to the parish priest. In a few weeks, I would write to the priest to give him an address where he should send the replies. A response came but it didn't bring any satisfactory result.

RICHMOND

I stayed only three days in Quebec. My feet were impatient to get to the Mr. Marin who lived in Richmond. I told myself, "This man must surely be my uncle, the father of Pierre who died at sea; he will give me definite news about my father, who is his brother."

Truly, I thought I would have no further trouble tracking down my relatives even after twenty-five years. I was then under the impression that Pierre Doucet was my first cousin while in reality we were only second cousins. I had no doubt whatsoever about the upcoming success of my efforts; my lack of success hadn't yet made me a pessimist.

I crossed the river at Pointe-Lévis and followed sometimes the king's highway, sometimes the Grand Trunk railroad line.[37] Unable to find lodging one night, I slept in a barn, buried up to my neck in a pile of straw. I was very cold.

"It doesn't matter," I told myself, "be patient. It will be warm at my uncle's, and I'll have a good bed to rest in."

Five days later, in the village of Richmond, I knocked at the door of a small, white house located southwest of the railroad tracks.

"Come in," said an old man with a gray beard. His wife sat near the stove, rocking herself and knitting.

I said, "Are you Mr. Marin?"

"Yes, my friend, at your service."

37. The Grand Trunk Railway started in 1852-53 to connect Montreal to Toronto and later Sarnia, Ontario to Portland, Maine. By 1867 the Grand Trunk became one of the largest railway systems in the world. Then the main railway system in Quebec and Ontario, its tracks spread to most cities in eastern Canada running as far west as Chicago, Illinois. In 1882, it added the Great Western Railway to its long list of railway acquisitions. In 1923, it became part of the Canadian National Railways. (Illus. *l'Opinion publique*, 23 Dec. 1875. Courtesy of BAnQ.)

"Have you lost a child?"

"Alas, yes," he replied with a deep sigh.

The blood stopped in my heart, I thought I would faint.

"You are my uncle!" I cried in a quavering voice and rushed forward to embrace him.

The old man, very moved, took my hand and held it in both of his. Startled, the old lady had risen and threw herself between us crying. I started to recount my story, but the old man interrupted me.

"I'm so sorry for you, my good friend, but I am not your uncle. It was a young daughter whom I lost and it wasn't twenty-five years ago."

Tears poured from his eyes. "Poor boy," he continued, "I pity you with all my heart, and I pity your parents even more for what has happened. It will soon be sixteen years since my little girl was kidnapped, and it's always in my memory as though it happened yesterday."

The lady sobbed so much that she started choking and fled into her bedroom.

"Stay with us for a while," said the old man, "get some rest and then at your leisure tell us the story of your life."

I was happy to accept; my feet were again full of blisters from the long walk. The good woman's salve was good for my sores and the old people's warm sympathy a balm for my heart.

ST. JEAN

I remained three days in Richmond. One of the neighbors who came——each night a great number of them gathered at the little, white house to see and hear the lost child ——told me he knew a few Marins in St.-Jean in Dorchester. I left for St.-Jean.

I followed the rail line as far as Beloeil, and from there took the king's highway that ran along the Richelieu River to my destination. Mr. Marin lived in the country, a mile and a half from the church. When I knocked at his door, he was eating dinner with his family.

"I haven't lost any children," he answered, "and you have the proof of that before your eyes in these dozen mouths assembled around my table. Among my relatives, I don't know anyone who has had this kind of misfortune."

I decided to go on to Montreal, thinking to myself, "In a big city it will be easier to get information."

I walked all night along a canal bank. When it was morning, I stopped in Chambly at a hotel run by a woman.

"Madam, would you be good enough to give me a some charity?"

"No, I don't give any charity to the lazy. You're young, work."

"Madam, could you give me some work?"

"Yes, go out in the yard and chop some wood."

Fasting as I was, I found the hatchet and the scythe heavy to wield. Half an hour later, the woman called to me through her partly opened doorway, "That's enough, friend, come and eat."

I understood that I was now in a densely populated center of bustle and commerce. In the far away countryside, people are so charitable that the right hand doesn't know what the left hand is doing. By contrast, in the populated villages and wealthy country-side that surrounds them, no one gives anything away for nothing—rather, it's an eye for an eye, a tooth for a tooth.

MONTREAL

I crossed from Longueuil to Montreal by steamboat. It was cold and  bands of ice (*bordages*)[38] had set along the river's edge. On board, I kept hearing that this was one of the steamer's last trips for the season.

During the next seven or eight days, I explored Montreal in every direction, lodging sometimes in one end of the city, sometimes in another, dining here, supping there. My money melted away like butter in a frying pan. I sought advice from police, shopkeepers, innkeepers, passers-by, and from the priests of the great parish.[39] They consulted their directories[40] and sent me to a number of Marins, one residing on such and such a street, another on another such street. Not one of them answered to the description I gave. Each night, I was tired from all my running around and discouraged from having turned up nothing. Montreal is a beautiful city, but I saw nothing of its monuments, its public squares, its parks and churches. A single thought absorbed my entire attention: to find the Marin who had lost two children.

I met a well-dressed man on the street whom I took to be a lawyer. I asked him my question.

"You should put a notice in the papers," he said. "Come with me."

38. "We call *bordage* the edge of ice that forms along the shore before the river totally freezes over." —J.-B. Proulx

39. "Popular name of the Notre-Dame parish, because for over two centuries it was the only parish for Montreal and its suburbs."—J.-B. Proulx

40. Fr. *directoires*: "Name of the almanac of streets and addresses in a city, a word that the Canadians translated from the English 'directory', which after all is as worthy as the Parisian word '*botin*'..."—J.-B. Proulx.

The earliest Canadian directory appeared in the 1780s for the city of Quebec, in 1819 for Montreal, and after the mid 1800s for other cities.

He led me to a newspaper office. One of the editors took notes from my dictation. When he was finished, he said, "This is good, you'll appear in tomorrow's edition."

I took out my wallet to pay him a dollar, as I had in Quebec.

"Hold on to your money, your story is far too interesting; we should be paying you."

Montreal did not live up to my expectations or exertions. One of the priests of Notre Dame parish had told me that many Marins lived on the outskirts of Ottawa. I decided to push on to this area.

## ON THE ROAD
## TO OTTAWA

I passed by Plouffe, St.-Martin, St.-Eustache, St.-Benoit, Pointe-aux-Anglais, and Carillon. It was cold and I was poorly dressed. Some nights I had to knock on five or six doors before finding shelter for the night. I knew then what it was like to be called "lazy," "shiftless," "a bum." It is true that my second-hand clothes and my habitually timid demeanor, hanging my head under every reproach, didn't make a very good impression. But in other situations, in order to satisfy peoples' whims to hear a recital of my adventures, I spent a whole day, even two days in the same house. Then a well-set table soothed my stomach, a good bed restored my constitution, and I enjoyed the delicious warmth of a nice stove.

Along the way, I asked about families named Marin. One night, someone told me, "One of them lives not far from here, on the road to Ottawa. He owns a hotel."

I don't remember the exact place where I was at that moment; it must have been around Calumet—there was a small mountain on my right. I had still three miles to go and it was growing dark. Snow was falling heavily; it was windy and cloudy with powdery snowflakes. I couldn't see more than two inches past my nose. I proceeded slowly. My shoes had holes in them and my feet were frozen.

Covered with snow, I entered the hotel. The owner was sitting down, placidly smoking his pipe.

"Sir, are you Mr. Marin?"

"Yes, I call myself simply Jean-Baptist Marin, without the Mister."

"My name is also Marin and I am looking for my parents."

I had hardly begun telling him about my kidnapping when he interrupted me saying, "Yes, yes, I know all that. You are a man looking to cadge a free meal. Get on your way, get on your way and leave at once."

Montreal to Morrisburg (1870–1874)

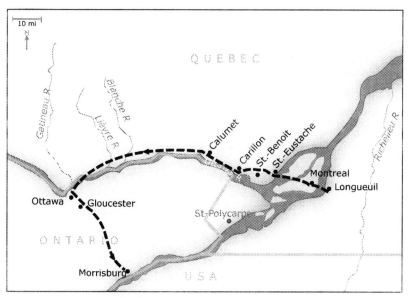

I sat down on the porch and wept, my poor feet refused to go any farther. A small boy of about seven came over to me and asked, "Why are you crying?"

"Dear child," I answered, "if you had the same bad luck as I, you'd be crying too. I am a lost child, stolen. I have no one in the world, no father, no mother, no friends. See my frozen feet, and now I'm thrown out the door like a dog."

The little boy ran to tell what I had said to his mother who had just come in from the barn carrying a pail of milk. The woman spoke to her husband, and the child came over to say, "Papa said to come in."

The woman placed a chair near the stove for me. She helped me remove my socks, then brought over a basin of cold water, and rubbed and dried my feet while saying to her husband, "The poor man must really be suffering."

"Oh," I thought to myself, "God bless this wonderful woman."

After supper, we all sat around the stove, the man with a pipe in his mouth, the woman with her two sons at her sides, one seven, the other nine.

"Where are you from?" asked the hotel owner.

"It would be difficult for me to tell you. I was stolen at the age of five, and I've forgotten the name of the place where I was born, if I ever knew it."

That said, I then began to tell them my history, from the beginning to the end. From time to time, I stopped, saying, "Give me a moment to rest, I can't go on, my feet are hurting too much."

The man listened in silence. The woman couldn't stop wiping her eyes on her apron, completely filling it with her tears.

She said to her two sons. "If you were like this poor man, without a father and mother, how sad you would be! What would you do? You have a good mother and you don't listen to her!"

The children sobbed. That night many tears were shed in Mr. Jean-Baptist Marin's house. At the end of the evening, I lay on the floor, completely worn out.

When her husband had gone to bed the woman came and prodded me, saying, "Young man, get up and follow me".

My shoes and stockings in hand, I followed her. My feet were so swollen that I could barely walk. She led me to the attic off the kitchen where she had prepared a soft bed near the chimney flue. I lay down and she covered me as she would a baby. This was the first time, since my kidnapping that I received these little attentions. I was touched to the bottom of my heart.

"Ah, if only my mother were like her," I thought, "then I would have such a good mother. But mine may be dead... or maybe she is still crying over my loss... How unfortunate I am!"

My feet made me suffer all night long. The next morning, they gave me breakfast. The woman would have gladly kept me there for a few days, but the man said nothing. I understood that it would be better for me to continue on my way. I thanked them over and over again and left with a heavy heart. The woman had tears in her eyes and the two boys shook my hand.


GLOUCESTER

In one push, I arrived in Ottawa, and spent two days in the capital. The Parliament buildings, the Cathedral with its grand proportions, the Chaudières, the Rideau Falls, all that held hardly any interest for me. I was under the sway of an *idée fixe* —enthralled, dominated, possessed. But no one I approached could give me any information. It was all very discouraging.

Finally, I met a man who told me, "There's definitely a man by the name of Marin in Gloucester. I seem to have heard it said that he lost an infant in some tragic way, although I am not entirely sure of this."

"How far is Gloucester from here?"

"About twelve miles."

"I thank you, Sir. It's noon, tonight I will sleep in Gloucester."

I started out at once, without having eaten. I had barely covered half the distance when I found myself on a deserted stretch of farm road (*montée*)[41] far from any houses. I felt weak, rather sick; I thought I was going to die. My legs were weakening, my head spinning, and all around me everything had turned yellow. I lost consciousness and collapsed.

When I came to, I was lying in a wagon, and a kind man was rubbing my hands and face with snow. I felt better and breathed easier, but my legs were cold and my feet frozen—more frozen than the first time.

"Who are you?" he asked.

"My name is Louis Marin."

"Where are you going?"

"I am looking for Mr. Marin, who, I am told, lives in Gloucester."

"That's true, he lives not far from here, I go within a half mile of his house."

---

41. "One calls a "*montée*" [rise, climb] the road that goes from one concession to another and consequently unites the two sections [hills/*côtes*], along which there are usually very few dwellings." —J.-B. Proulx

Like "*côte*," "*montée*" is used regardless of whether the terrain is hilly or flat. For example, today there is a Montée Cholette, the road running along the present day Cholette family farm in St.-Polycarpe.

This good Samaritan wanted to take me right to his door.

"No, no," I told him, "I will not allow you to go out of your way for me. Besides, this short walk will warm me up and do me good. Thank you, my dear Sir. Without you, I would be a dead man."

I found Mr. Marin, at the back of his house, his face black with soot, hacking away at half-burnt wood, which is abundant on new lands. He was an old man, past his sixtieth year.

"Are you Mr. Marin?" I inquired.

"Yes, I am called Louis Marin."

I felt a shiver; he had my name! "Have you lost any children?"

"Yes and no, it depends. First, I never had any children, but I did raise an orphan whom I loved like a son. He was horribly crushed by a falling tree."

"In that case, you are not the man I am looking for. I am a lost child, kidnapped at the age of five; and now I'm traveling all over the country to find my father."

"Come in anyway, it's nighttime and you can't sleep outside. We'll see about all that."

I didn't have to be begged. I sat against the stove, my body shivering, my teeth chattering. His wife brought me a basin of cold water to thaw my feet in. I was unable to keep myself from making a thousand contortions and grimaces from the pain.

The good woman questioned me at great length about my adventures and about how I came to their house.

I told her, "There is a man in Ottawa who told me that your husband was my father, and at your second neighbor's, where I stopped to warm myself, all agreed that Mr. Marin must be a relative of mine because I resemble him a lot."

She seemed agitated and upset.

"That's very true," she said, "you do resemble him. We never had any family, but he did a lot of running around. He was a raft pilot[42] and traveled all his life."

"Madam," I said, "you are wrong to want to pass your husband off as a man of weak character."

The old fellow, who sat on the other side of the stove, kept silent quietly laughing up his sleeve.

"That's good, friend, come have supper with us. You are in no shape to continue your journey. Spend a few days with us, and we'll see how things turn out."

The old woman was shocked. She sulked and grumbled under her breath as she washed the dishes.

At nine o'clock, we went to bed. I could hear the old couple arguing.

"You're heartless, why do you need to keep this stranger here for nothing?"

"You are always the same," he replied. "You don't like to be charitable."

"Yes, to the poor, but not to the lazy."

"Who's to say that this man is lazy? You can see that he can hardly walk.

42. Raft pilot (*guide des cages*): "The *cage* [called "booms" in the old Adirondack lumber industry] is a raft made out of logs which the lumbermen leave to the river's currents to carry it to market; the *guide* is the pilot who directs the rowers how to follow the direction of the current." —J.-B. Proulx

Illus.: "Cages on the St. Lawrence." *Le Monde illustré*, 15 April 1893. Courtesy of BAnQ.

If you were in his place, would you want someone to throw you out?"

"Ah ha! I can plainly see that he's your son!"

The old man said no more.

"Now wait," I said, "don't quarrel because of me. I can go to one of your neighbors and ask for shelter, until my feet are well enough to continue on my journey."

"Don't worry, my friend," replied the old man, "this storm will pass. I'm used to her fits of temper. It's been forty years of quarreling and, as you can see, I'm bearing up pretty well."

The old woman kept quiet.

My feet healed but I didn't leave right away. I helped Mr. Marin prepare new ground, fell trees, cut them into eight to ten foot lengths, put them into piles and burn them. With the return of spring, I spread seeds with a thorny harrow in and around the tree stumps. The woman became well disposed towards me and treated me like a son.

I had never been to church so often in whole my life. Every two weeks a priest came and said Mass in a neighboring house that temporarily served as a chapel. Since I could read, I recited the response for the Mass from my book, and served Mass. By taking on the duties of a sacristan, I gained the respect of these people.

In the month of June, I decided to resume my quest. Two days before my departure, I found Mr. Marin seated before the fireplace his head in his hands, deep in thought (*jongleux*).[43]

" Father, what are you thinking about so much?"

"Louis," he said, lifting his head and looking into my eyes, "why

43. *"Jongleux*, in our rural areas, has a pensive connotation. Jugglers [*jongleurs*], our homespun sorcerers, would affect serious or philosophical airs." —J.-B. Proulx

leave? Haven't you been well treated here? Stay with us. I am not rich, but you will not lose out for your trouble. I feel old; I have no children. Someday I will be giving my land to someone willing to pay me a pension.[44] Stay, who knows what may happen."

I found these propositions attractive, generous, but a bit too vague. "Thank you, Mr. Marin, but I find it impossible to stay any longer. I wanted to spend spring seeding time with you in order to repay you a little for your kindness in taking me in this winter when I was in bad shape. But an inner voice keeps urging me on, in spite of myself, to find my parents."

"You're wrong, you're wrong," repeated the old man. "You are wasting your time and sacrificing your future. You would do better to find a good home and save something up for your old age."

When I left, the old woman was crying; we had become completely reconciled. She embraced me saying, "Good-bye and good luck. Don't forget the Blessed Virgin."


MR. LOGAN'S

I walked along thinking over the old man's words, "You're wrong, you're wrong." These two phrases kept echoing in my ears like two bells.

"Maybe he's right," I thought. "My parents might have died a long time ago. Who still wonders about the poor little orphans? Our kidnapping certainly didn't make much noise back then; news of it didn't spread beyond the parish limits. Three small children were lost in the woods, they died of hunger, the wolves finished

44. "to give one's possessions to someone for a remuneration of an annual pension . This payment, often in kind, is determined by a gift contract [*contrat de donation*]." —J.-B. Proulx

them off; that's all. Our mothers cried over our graves, but strangers quickly forgot us. It's obvious that memory of us didn't stretch across a quarter of a century to reach the present generation. Here I am in western French Canada, it's just as likely that my parents live in the east, on the coast. After such a long journey, after all my fruitless efforts, my conscience needn't bother me. I will not be lacking in filial responsibility if I stop for a while to think about myself. I can't always live the life of a vagabond."

A man in a wagon caught up to me and said, "Get in, the friend."

I didn't make him repeat his invitation. He was an Englishman who spoke French rather poorly.

As we rode along, he asked, *"Vous savoir lire?"**

"Yes."

"Write?"

" A little."

*"Vous vouloir engager vous pour enseigner école à mes garçonnes?"†*

*"Oui, moi vouloir!"*** I jumped at this opportunity considering it a stroke of providence. This man's name was James Logan; he lived in Bell's Corner.†† At his home I had an easy life, having only three small boys in my "school." In between class times, I harnessed the carriage, ran errands, and drove the lady of the house around.

At the end of my year there, I found I had reached the end of my knowledge of Latin. I didn't have a practiced enough hand to make my pupils progress any further in penmanship. My knowledge of spelling didn't permit me to push them any further in grammar. But in good conscience, I don't think they had wasted

---

\* "You to know to read?"

† "You to want to engage you to teach school to my boy-sies?"

\*\* "Yes, me to want to!"

†† Could not locate Bell's Corner.

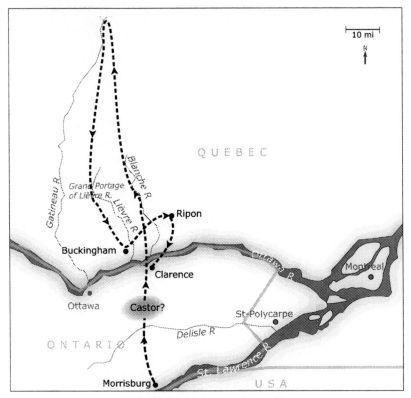

Morrisburg to Clarence (1874-1876)

their time. In twelve months, I had taught them to speak and read French fairly well. After vacation, the three of them left for the big schools.

Mr. Logan had a first class hotel in Morrisburg to rent out. He asked me, "You, to want to come with me to take care of my court-yard and stables? Me to give to you the same pay as for school."

I followed him to Morrisburg, where I spent the next two years. My job consisted of harnessing and unharnessing visitors' horses and meeting the arriving trains four times a day to pick up travelers.

My salary was ten dollars a month, but gentlemen's tips brought me more. Where did all that money go? I don't know; I didn't drink or gamble. It's a great misfortune not having a father or guardian to teach you from childhood how to economize.

Mr. Logan and his family were Protestants. Sometimes they would talk to me about their religion, and they wanted to take me to their meetings (*mitaine*).[45] I went twice out of curiosity, but I found it boring. I was not then what you would call a fervent Catholic; but I never missed saying my prayers each morning and night. As if by instinct, I often sought help from the Blessed Virgin and I have no doubt that I am obligated to her for having survived so many perils and setbacks.

I never stopped thinking about my parents. During these three restful years, the thought of them followed me around like a shadow, often like a reproach. After returning to my room at night, I would hear a voice say, "Don't you have any spirit? Do you always want to remain a stranger on this earth? Where are your good resolutions? You let yourself be discouraged by the first few obstacles. Try again, the reward for perseverance is success."

Hardly a week went by that I did not try to get information from travelers about my family. One day someone told me, "You don't have far to go, in Castor or thereabouts you will find a family named Marin."

My three years were over. In June, I gave Mr. Logan my notice and set out to find fame and fortune.

---

45. "Name that the Canadians gave to Protestant assemblies, from the English word 'meeting.'"—J.-B. Proulx

CASTOR

After a couple of days walking I arrived at the church in Castor.* I went to see the pastor—he being the best-informed person in the village.

"My friend," he said, "you have been misinformed, there is no one in my parish by the name of Marin."

At that moment, the church warden entered. He offered to take me to his home six miles away. I spent eight days at his house. Each night, neighborhood people gathered at his home to hear me tell my story. The miseries I had suffered moved them all to pity and I became celebrated in those parts.

At the end of my stay, one of the neighbors, who had attended every night without fail and who generally listened quietly, spoke to me earnestly, "My poor friend, I am sorry for you. You're wasting your time running all around the world, and you're making yourself miserable. You look like a good man; settle down and you will succeed. Would you like to come and stay with us for a while? I will treat you like a son."

His words sounded wise, and the look on his face was so sincere and kind that I said, "Very good, I'll happily take you up on your offer, or challenge. But first I must warn you, that apart from harnessing a horse and harrowing around tree stumps, I don't know how to do very much."

"You're young, you'll learn."

The man's name was Pierre Sigouin. He had seven daughters, the oldest being twenty and the youngest six, but not a single son.

*Could not find Castor on current maps but there is a Castor River where a possible location of Castor is indicated on the map, p. 102.

I stayed with the family through the summer, autumn and winter—almost a year. I learned how to reap and thresh. These were some of the best people on earth such as you rarely meet, always in good spirits, honest, church-going people. Each night we prayed together; every Sunday two wagons were at our disposal to take us to Mass. We rarely spent a month without going to confession and communion. Vagabond as I had been all my life, I was a Catholic more in name than in fact. At Mr. Sigouin's I saw the light, I realized the truth, and I embraced the Christian faith, which I hope will stay with me for as long as I live. I can never be able to thank the Lord enough for letting me fall into such a good household.

Nowhere else has given me so many good memories. Here is one that I can't resist telling.

On the first of April, while we were having breakfast, Mr. Langlois entered and said, "Louis, could you do me a small favor? Yesterday, I was in the village with the pastor and I left at his place a brand new tirepoke and hallepoke that I had just bought."

"What did you call them?"

"A tirepoke and a hallepoke."

I looked at him. He didn't laugh. I cast a scrutinizing eye over my table companions. Everyone's face was serene and serious. The words sounded funny. But I thought there are still some tools whose names I don't know. As I had been raised at sea, I was ignorant of so many things on land.

"That's okay," I replied, "I'll gladly go."

He gave me his sleigh (*sleigh d'officier*)[46] and his beautiful fat horse, which behaved like a team of four in harness. Flying over

46. "Sleigh, an English word that has passed into Canadian French as steamboat has passed into French. The experts have the noun as masculine, while the people give it as feminine. *Sleigh d'officier*: a sleigh mounted high on its runners." —J.-B. Proulx

the road like a speck of dust, I arrived at the rectory in the wink of an eye.

"Pastor, I've come for Mr. Langlois' tirepoke and hallepole."

Without answering me, he dashed into the next room, and I heard someone splitting his sides in laughter. He quickly returned, his face wreathed in smiles. "That's true, Mr. Langlois left them here, but this is a bad turn of events. He had to send his horse and carriage…and then you who have lost a morning."

"Oh," I said, "it's nothing; my time is not precious."

The Pastor was chuckling all the while. I felt bad for Mr. Langlois who must have made a really big blunder.

He called his servant. Without my knowing it, they had wrapped three bundles of kindling wood in newspaper, tied them securely, and stuffed them into the bag I had brought.

"Carry this carefully," he said, "it's somewhat fragile."

I departed with the "tirepoke" upright between my two legs. I heard a roar of laughter behind me. Innocent as a newborn babe, I suspected nothing; this was staggering considering the trouble I then had. The road was full of bumps and the horse, irritated and confused, raced over them. He nearly got the bit between his teeth and the effort to rein him in made my arms numb, not to mention, that at each bounce, I worried that the hallepoke or tirepoke would break into pieces. Covered in sweat and out of sorts I arrived back home. Imagine my surprise when I saw everybody, men, women and children, coming out the door holding knives and forks, and a frying pan in preparation for roasting the *April fish.* I pretended to be angry but in my heart I was glad. "People," I said to myself, "only play jokes like this on their friends."

**April Fools Day/*Poisson d'Avril***

April

1

The origin of April Fools Day—in France called "*le poisson d'avril*" (April fish)— began in 1562 with the new Gregorian (after Pope Gregory XIII) calendar, which moved the start of the New Year from April 1st to January 1st. Because diehards and those who didn't hear about the new calendar continued to celebrate April 1st as the New Year, a tradition grew of celebrating April 1st by giving false presents and playing jokes and tricks like sending people on "fool's errands." This tradition may have begun in France because King Charles IX was one of the first rulers to adopt the new calendar in 1564. Explanations for why in France the fish became the symbol for April Fool's Day are less clear. Here are a few: because April 1st occurs towards the end of Lent when eating meat was prohibited; because, on the other hand that is around the time when fish reproduce, and fishing was prohibited; because it's when the moon leaves the zodiacal sign of the fish; because it was easy to draw a fish sign and stick it on someone's back.

I MET A YOUNG MAN who talked me into going up the Blanche River to work in a phosphate mine. I committed the folly of leaving a place where I was so well off. It is said that each life has an evil hour; this was mine.

"You're making a mistake," Mrs. Sigouin said. "Here you eat well, sleep well, you are happy, you earn good wages. Why go running after trouble?"

"You're right," I replied. "But what can I do? My longing for parents, which was slumbering for a while, has reawakened again

"A crew of lumbermen posing for a photograph." *L'Album universel,* 30 January 1904. Courtesy of BAnQ.

stronger than ever and follows me everywhere. Maybe when traveling and working around the country, I will have the opportunity to hear some news about them."

When leaving, I went to kiss them good-bye. Mr. Sigouin shook my hand without saying a word. The youngest children hung onto my clothes; the wife and older girls were crying and sobbing. I'm not sure who wept more, they or I.

THE BLANCHE RIVER

We hired ourselves out to a Mr. Miller at a salary of a dollar and a half a day. The boss asked me, "Do you know how to cook?"

"Yes," I told him, "I learned this trade as a boy when I sailed the high seas."

He gave me a big apron, which was white once upon a time, and there I was installed as chef and cook's helper all in one. Having to prepare and cook meals for twenty or so men was not a picnic; but it was better than crushing and loading ore. I was rejoicing at my good fortune when, fifteen days later, the mine operation shut down. The workers found themselves out on the street, all without work and several without pay. I was one of the latter.

I spent the rest of the summer in the area, around Maskinongé Lake,* at a widow's by the name of Montreuil, who had no one to work on her land but her little boy and girl. I took care of the fields and harvesting. At the first snowfall, I wanted to settle my accounts with her. She said that she owed me nothing. I took legal action against her but lost. It seemed our agreement was poorly made. Fortunately, my lawyer had taken the case on a fifty-fifty basis for I hadn't a penny to give him. Ever since I had left Mr. Sigouin's, nothing much had entered my pockets, and they remained empty.

After losing my lawsuit, I was walking along aimlessly in the village, with my head down, my hands behind my back, sad as a whipped dog, when I ran into a man who asked me, "Are you still searching for your parents"?

"Yes!"

"Have you been to see a Mr. Marin who lives at the top the Gatineau River?

"No, is it far to get there?"

"Ninety miles."

"Thank you, Sir, I'm leaving tomorrow."

When I thought about having to travel ninety miles on foot, over snow-covered roads and mountains, I felt fainthearted. "Bah!" I said to myself, "after all, I will earn at least as much as I did this summer. Let's go."

*Couldn't locate a Maskinongé Lake in this area.

## THE GATINEAU RIVER

It took me three weeks to go those ninety miles. The roads were horribly bad, snowdrifts rose as high as houses, storms stopped me in my tracks. I arrived about midday at Mr. Marin's house. I knocked on the door."

"Come in."

"Does Mr. Marin live here?"

" Marin is my name."

"Have you lost any children?"

After saying those words I felt faint and fell into a chair; the room seemed to be spinning.

"You are very pale, stranger. Are you sick?"

"No, but I am very tired. I can tell you that it's been very painful having to walk along the roads in this part of the country. The further north you go, the poorer people get, or else meaner. Last evening I knocked on eight doors without being able to get anything to eat, and at the ninth I was given shelter in the barn."

"So you went to bed without any supper?"

"No. The woman had told me, 'There isn't any bread in the bin and we are finished making loaves to bake.' I waited for a batch of bread to be almost done baking and, slipping through the shadows in back of the oven, I took away a loaf. Hidden under my bed of straw, I wolfed it down while it was still fresh and warm. I haven't had such a meal for the last three weeks."

"Where are you bound for?"

"I'm looking for my parents. I am a child of the Marins; I was kidnapped when I was five years old. If you are my father, please tell me because I've been traveling for so long to find you."

"I am certainly not your father. I know a Marin who lives at the grand portage of the Lièvre River, eighteen miles north of Buckingham, where he runs a sort of hotel for the *voyageurs* work-

**Voyageurs** were the men, most often French Canadians, who manned the canoes for the three large fur trading companies: the Hudson's Bay Company, the Northwest Company and the later American Fur Company (started by John Jacob Astor in 1808). *Voyageurs* were most active from the mid 1700s until the mid 1800s when the fashion for beaver hats in Europe declined and consequently so too did the fur trade, Canada's first industry. Via waterways and portage, *voyageurs* traveled tens of thousands of miles from Montreal to the Canadian west, as well as into present-day Illinois, Michigan and Minnesota (which today boasts a Voyageur National Park and a Voyageurs Highway).

*Voyageurs* would paddle for sixteen or more hours a day in cramped canoes over rivers and rapids, carry (portage) canoes and supplies over long, rough trails between waterways, and camp out in the wilderness in all kinds of weather; it greatly helped to be young, healthy, and short of stature. In these lightweight, birch bark canoes, *voyageurs* transported goods like guns, clothing, fabric, and pots to trade for furs with First Nations people. While they paddled and carried heavy weights, they kept up their spirits and teamwork with song; there are hundreds of *voyageur* songs.

In his travelogue *Astoria*, Washington Irving described the distinctive clothing of the *voyageurs* he saw working for Astor's American Fur Company in the early 1800s:

> The dress of these people is generally half-civilized half-savage. They wear a capot or surcoat, made of a blanket, a striped cotton shirt, cloth trousers, or leathern leggings, moccasins of deer skin, and a belt of variegated worsted, from which are suspended the knife, tobacco pouch, and other instruments...

"En route to Hudson's Bay." *Le Monde illustré*, 16 July 1887. Courtesy of BAnQ

Most *voyageurs* retired to their homeland in Quebec, but many remained with their First Nations wives living as trappers and small farmers in the Canadian and U.S. West (see boxed text on p. 62).

A Canadian historian observed in 1914:

Men of extraordinary endurance and great courage, the voyageurs have performed useful work in the interests of civilization, if not their own; they have also contributed to build the fortunes of Hudson's Bay and Northwest lords of the forest, and of our wealthy lumbermen. Their great fault was... that they were satisfied to take things as they found them.*

A retired *voyageur* in his seventies reflected back on his hard life, where he made no fortune for himself, but had no regrets:

I could carry paddle, walk and sing with any man I ever saw. I have been twenty-four years a canoe man, and forty-one years in service; no portage was ever too long for me. Fifty songs could I sing. I have saved the lives of ten voyageurs. I have had twelve wives and six run-ning dogs. I spent all my money in pleasure. Were I young again, I should spend my life the same way over. There is no life so happy as a voyageur's life!**

Proulx didn't see a need to footnote the term *voyageur, but* today's standard French dictionaries as well as bilingual dictionar-ies published in France or Canada do not provide the historical definition of *voyageur*; "*voyageur*" is simply defined as "traveler," or "commercial traveler." Standard U.S. dictionaries, however, do supply its historical meaning, e.g.: "[Fr. traveler] in Canada, a) a person who transported goods and men by boat to trading posts for the fur companies."*** Voyageurs were first called *coureurs de bois* (woods runners) and later with the founding of the North-west Company, when they became licensed and regulated by the government, they became known as *voyageurs du pays en haut* or just *voyageurs*.

*Adam Shortt and Arthur G. Doughty, eds., Vol. 15 of *Canada and Its Provinces: A History of the Canadian People and Their Institutions by One Hundred Associates,* (Toronto: T. & A. Constable, 1913-17) 73, 78.
**James H. Baker, "Lake Superior," *Minnesota Historical Collections*, 3:342, quoted in Grace Lee Nute's fine book, *The Voyageur*, Reprint Edition (St. Paul: Minnesota Historical Society, 1955) vi.
***Webster's New World College Dictionary*, 4th Edition.

ing around there. Maybe he's one of your relatives."

"Oh," I cried, "how unhappy I am. I will never have a place on this earth."

"My friend," replied Mr. Marin, "stay here as long as you want. The table is set, come and eat. You will have supper with us; you will spend the night under my roof. Young man, let yourself completely recover from your exhaustion."

I stayed with this good man until noontime two days later.

### THE GRAND PORTAGE
### OF THE LIÈVRE

Near the end of January three weeks later, during the most severe winter weather, I arrived at the grand portage of the Lièvre River. I had walked far and was worn out. The night's long shadows were spreading over the forest. Every now and then, through the fall-

"Portage between two rivers, en route to Manitoba." *L'Opinion publique*, 5 Oct. 1871. Courtesy of BAnQ. See the canoe on the left being hauled uphill on log rails.

ing snowflakes, I could see the flickering lights of the hotel. Then a gust of powdery snow would plunge me into darkness again. Coming from the direction of the hotel, I heard the cries of men carousing and arguing. I entered and the seven or eight *voyageurs* who had been clamoring at the bar suddenly fell silent and glared at me with hostility. I trembled like a leaf.

A strapping, six-foot fellow with large, square shoulders lumbered over to me and in a haughty voice demanded, "What do you want?"

"Is a Mr. Marin here?"

"Yes, that's me, and I'm not afraid of any man."

I knew they were all hotheads. "Me, too," I continued, "my name is Marin, I was kidnapped when I was five years old and I am searching for my parents."

"You won't find them here. And another thing, see, you are not the first to come to me with a long tale of woe, expecting me to feed him and lodge him. When a man asks me for charity in the name of God, I give it to him. But when he tries to fool me with a trumped-up story, I show him the door without further ceremony. My friend, you know how you came in, you can leave the same way."

"Sir, won't you consider that no one can survive outdoors in this kind of weather?"

"Leave, I'm telling you, leave."

I didn't budge. He lunged at me, grabbed me by the scruff of my neck and the seat of my pants, and, seasoning his gesture with a good kick, sent me sailing across the room like a boxing glove. I lay there for some minutes, stunned, unable to get up. I could hear them laughing, jeering, sneering, squabbling. Dear God, what a mess I had gotten into.

Exhausted, I went back to the road that went through the woods. Nine miles separated me from the nearest settlement. I was afraid of the wolves; it seemed that at any moment I would see their fiery eyes blazing at me from the depths of the underbrush. I listened anxiously; I heard only the wind whistling through the treetops, and from time to time the faint echoes of shouts and curses escaping from the hotel. Disheartened and afraid, my hair standing on end, I fell to my knees in the snow and prayed.

"Dear God, don't abandon me, because I am going to die in this forest and even passers-by won't find my body buried under a mountain of snow."

I had barely dragged myself three miles when I heard behind me noises of something approaching. Terrified, my ears pricked up, I stood still. Soon I could discern the clear, silvery sounds of bells. A man in a wagon caught up to me. I asked if I could ride with him a bit.

"Okay," he said, "get in."

About a quarter of a mile farther on, the road started sloping down toward the river. Not paying any attention to this and going at a good clip, we drove headlong into a hole in the river's ice—the current had eaten away the underside of the ice until only a thin layer of snow and ice remained on the surface. The horse and wagon slid into the abyss never to be seen again while the man and I struggled in the broken ice. The water was cold—though not as much as you might imagine—but my fingers were freezing from trying to hold on to the floating chunks of ice. After many attempts, I finally managed to hoist myself onto a solid portion. Grabbing my companion by the shoulder, I pulled him up beside me. I acted just in time, for his strength was gone and he was about to drown.

In the midst of this, we heard another wagon approaching. I ran to meet it, shouting, "Don't come this way, we just drowned our animal."

The new arrival had a double team of horses. We unhitched the two horses, and led them by the bridle, one by one, in a long circle past the dangerous spot; then we pulled the wagon around by hand. During this time, the man who had lost his horse was ranting and raving, running here and there, tearing his hair out, and wanting to throw himself in the water.

"Come with us," the man with the two horses said to him. "It's useless to look any longer; the current has carried everything away and will not bring anything back. Of course, this is a great loss to you, but, still, you should consider yourself lucky to be alive."

We traveled the rest of the night. I was frozen. From time to time we ran behind the wagon in order to warm ourselves. But with our clothes frozen stiff as boards, it was very awkward to jog along. At six o'clock in the morning, we entered the village of Buckingham. I thanked the driver for having brought me there, and the other man thanked me for pulling him out of the river. Both of them wished me good luck in my search.

"Thank you, thank you!" Shaking hands, we separated. In only a few hours, a common danger and mutual aid had made us fast friends.

BUCKINGHAM

I went straight to the rectory. The pastor was just leaving to say Mass. In a few words I told him about my accident the night before and asked him for any information.

He said, "Very well, go to the kitchen, they will give you clothes to change into. Warm yourself and have breakfast, after Mass we'll talk about your situation."

Around nine o'clock he called me into his office. He cross-examined me at great length and wore me down with endless questions. I wanted to leave.

"I can't take up any more of your time and abuse your patience."

"Don't worry," he said, "I find this very interesting. Besides, you can't leave now; you have to wait until your clothes are dry, because," he added laughing, "I'm not giving you mine. After dinner if you wish you may continue on your journey. Until then you are my prisoner."

He seemed to take a great interest in my problems. "There is no one named Marin around here in Buckingham. Maybe you will find someone in Ripon; people living in that canton come from many different parishes in Canada. I will give you a letter of recommendation for the pastor there."

I was confused and touched by so much kindness. When I was leaving, I threw myself on my knees to thank him and ask for his blessing.

He pulled me up and embraced me saying, "You are a good, young man and God will bless you. You will find your parents. You will find them when you least expect it."

RIPON

I left for Ripon. "You will find your parents" These words resonated in my ears like a prophecy. This priest seemed to me to be inspired by God; he spoke with such fervor and assurance. I would find my parents, I was convinced of it; I felt repaid for all my suffering. With an unshakable optimism, I awaited the immediate ful-

"Lumbermen's rustic dwelling (*chantier*)." *L'Album universel*, 30 January 1904. Courtesy of BAnQ.

fillment of this promise. Indeed, it would be realized, but only on its own complete terms: *when I least expected it.*

I proceeded with a joyful heart but on tired legs. The night I spent without sleep, the accident I experienced, the freezing I endured, the different emotions that had come to assail me, one after another, all this wore down my resilience. At dusk I knocked at a small house to ask for shelter for the love of God.

"Yes," replied a woman, still young, but emaciated, "I can gladly give you a place to sleep, but I can't give you any supper, for we have nothing to eat in the house."

I approached the blazing hearth. Five thin, pale, gaunt children, the eldest being twelve years old, were huddled around the fire. It would be impossible to be poorer than this family. In this one room house, I saw neither table, nor bed, nor chairs. The three smallest boys were crying all the time, saying, "Mama, I'm so hungry, mama, some bread." It was heartbreaking. All the same, I slept on the uneven floorboards.

I awoke the next morning hungry as a wolf. But I couldn't find anything to eat all that morning. The houses were few and far between along the road I traveled and they were just shanties, crude cabins *(chantiers)*,[47] almost as miserable as the one where I had just

47. "In new land, we call a *chantier* [shanty] a dwelling constructed of dovetailed logs, each grooved log fitting into the other." —J.-B. Proulx

The log cabin he is describing here seems similar to the type of shanty Cholet encountered earlier, see footnote 34, p. 80.

spent the night. At noontime, I was ready to drop. The trees were dancing before my eyes as if in a mirage. I knocked at the door of an English farmer, who lived in a fairly nice looking house. Upon entering, I collapsed. The Englishman helped me to my feet and asked if I were sick.

"I think," I said, "I am so feeble because I haven't eaten since midday yesterday."

He gave me a good meal. "Now," he said, "wouldn't you like to lie down a bit?"

Yes, please, I think a short nap would do me good."

He made up a bed for me near the stove. I fell asleep as soon as I lay down. When I awoke it was nighttime. I felt much better, but not too strong.

"Are you going to let me spend the night under your roof?"

"Certainly, we don't put people out, especially when they are sick. French, English, Catholic, Protestant, we are all brothers in Jesus Christ."

"Thanks," I said, "thanks, your charity is very comforting."

I was the Englishman's guest for eight days. When I was strong again, he said, "I have to do some business with one of my brothers, would you like to come along? We will go around Lake Ripon. Maybe there you can get news of your parents, which wouldn't be such a miracle"

"On the contrary," I said, "it would be a big miracle."

We went around the lake, stopping at several places to make inquiries, but none had any news of a Marin. I wasn't surprised, I had expected as much.

The next day, I took the hand of my benefactor saying, "Goodbye, Sir, Madam, I owe you a great deal. I leave healed in two ways: here I have found health and wisdom."

"How? What are you trying to say?"

"I've made the wise resolution to abandon my futile search forever."

"In our opinion, you are doing the right thing."

"Goodbye."

"So long."

7

*My Searches Stopped*

THE RETURN
OF THE
PRODIGAL SON

*I* went towards Clarence, on the south shore of the Ottawa River, and thought to myself, "How well off I had been at my father's house—I mean at Pierre Sigouin's. How foolish I had been to leave. Castor is not far away, why not go back? I will say to him, 'Dear Sir, I was wrong; will you forgive me? Will you take me in again like one of your children?' If he says, 'Your mania of roaming the world will return and you will leave us again,' I will answer, 'Have no fear, my resolution is not like the ones I made before. Like a seed of hope deep in my heart, there always used to be a secret desire to continue my search in opportune moments. Today, I feel dazed, completely disillusioned, literally disgusted. Frankly, I can't understand how I was able to take the words of the pastor in

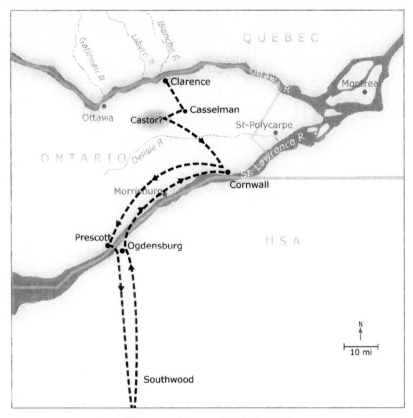

Clarence to Cornwall (1876-1879)

Buckingham for a prophecy; it was simply a wish made out of kindness. The cold bath of the night before must have deranged me. No, my parents are dead, or they live very far from here. It's obvious that God doesn't want me to find them. May his blessed will be done! After all, I have much to be thankful for—he has given back to me my most important possession of all: my freedom.'"

However, I didn't go to Castor right away. I was ashamed. My clothes were in rags and I didn't want to reappear at the Sigouin's looking far less shipshape than when I left. In order to get new

clothes I worked for five months—which seemed a long time—
first in Clarence in a sawmill, then in Casselman at a rich man's
house where I took care of four stallions. After that, I went on
my way, sharply dressed from head to toe in new clothes. It was
a beautiful summer day. I walked along with a spring to my step.
My heart as was gay as the sun shining brightly on me and as the
birds singing in the trees. All the pleasant memories of my past
came flooding back; I was going to live again in an atmosphere of
tranquillity, peace, joy and affection for all!

When I approached the house, my heart was beating so fast
that my chest threatened to burst. I knocked and a stranger appeared.

"Isn't this where Mr. Pierre Sigouin lives?"

"This used to be Mr. Sigouin's, but he's moved away."

"Since when?"

"Since last spring."

"Why did he sell? It seemed to me that his affairs were in order."

"Having no sons and his health not being good, farming became too hard for him. He had to find an easier way to make a
living."

"Where did he go?"

"To Cornwall. His older girls are working in a cotton mill, and
he does odd jobs with his horse and wagon."

Remorse stabbed my heart. If I had stayed with him, Mr.
Sigouin wouldn't have had to sell his land.

I left feeling very sad; it was midday. I went to Mr. Langlois's
who was happy to see me and wanted me to stay at least until the
next day.

"Thank you," I said. "Under other circumstances I would gladly accept your invitation but today I am in too much of a hurry to
see my benefactor." I left right after dinner.

123

One night, I had a great deal of trouble finding a place to sleep. At the first house I tried, someone answered, "We can't let you in, we have smallpox in the house." I went to the house next door, "We have smallpox." At the second neighbor's, again, "We have the pox."

Finally, I cried out, "Smallpox or not, if you will allow me to come in, I will stay the night."

"Very well, you may stay here."

When I saw the smallpox[48], the blood froze in my veins. I remained transfixed like a statue. Good God, I thought, if I, who have no relatives, catch this sickness, who will take care of me?

The table was set; the master invited me to come to it.

"Thank you!" I said, "but I don't feel up to it; I want to sleep more than I want to eat."

He told his wife to fix me a bed

"No need to do that," I quickly responded, "I am accustomed to sleeping on the ground, using my hat as a pillow."

After saying my prayers, which I said with more devotion than usual, asking God to preserve me from this dreaded disease, I stretched out on the floor near the hearth.

I awoke around five in the morning. I made my way to the door on tiptoe, silently opened it, and, without saying good-bye to anyone, took to the open spaces. The air was fresh and pure, how easily I breathed! Having reached a small, wooded area fragrant

48. Smallpox may have killed more humans than any other infectious disease on record. Long in existence, Europeans brought it to the New World in the 1500s and its spread greatly contributed to the decimation of native populations by more than 90%. In Montreal in Cholet's day, the largest outbreaks of smallpox occurred in 1855-1857 and in 1885. Although vaccination existed since the 1700s, in the 1800s it was not always either available or trusted. Cases of smallpox persisted in Canada until 1946 and in the world until 1977.

with morning scents, its foliage heavy with dew, I threw myself on my knees and said my morning prayers, "Thank you, my Lord, thank you! You have been so good to me. If I have gone through some bad days in my life, you have also given me wonderful times." When I thought I would arrive this very day at Mr. Sigouin's house, I was full of gratitude, my heart radiant, my step light.

MY FIRST STAY IN
CORNWALL

It was seven in the evening when, incognito, I made my entrance into Cornwall. I went first to the Plamondon Hotel and, half-fearful, half-hopeful, I asked the hotel owner if he knew of a Mr. Sigouin in his vicinity.

"Yes," he said, "I know of such a man who has built a house in the eastern part of the village."

"Do you know where he came from?"

"From Castor."

"That's just the man I am looking for."

He told his small son to show me the way.

I knocked and a twelve-year-old girl opened the door; she did not recognize me.

"Is your father in?"

"Yes, Sir."

Mr. Sigouin, who had heard us talking, appeared. As soon as he saw me he gave a loud shout. "It's Louis Marin, my dear, it's really Louis who has come back to us!"

She came running. "Is it really you, Louis?"

All the girls showed up, one after the other; they jumped on my neck, and the youngest sat on my lap. The whole family was as happy as if a son and brother had returned.

"Where did you come from?" asked Mrs. Sigouin.

"I came from the Blanche, the Gatineau, the Lièvre, Buckingham, Clarence, and twenty other places, whose names I've forgotten."

"Like the Wandering Jew, you did a lot of walking," she said.

"Yes, and I didn't always have five cents in my pocket."

"You must have been through a lot of hardships?"

"Madam, more than I can say."

"If you had stayed with us, you would have been much better off."

"Madam, I have regretted leaving often, very often."

"After you left, I often used to wake up in the middle of the night and I would wake up my husband to say, 'Poor Louis, he must be sleeping outdoors tonight; he would be so reluctant to ask for shelter.'"

"That's true, Madam. More than once, I slept under the stars; more than twenty times I went the whole day without eating. Then I thought of you people, and would say to myself what a fool I was to have left such a good place and such a nice family."

On hearing this, Mrs. Sigouin began to cry, followed by Mr. Sigouin, and the children; we all cried and laughed together.

Mrs. Sigouin continued, "All that you've been saying we had predicted to you, not that we wished it, because you don't deserve anyone to wish you ill, and you were such a great help to us, the year you spent with us."

"Stay with us now," Mr. Sigouin said.

"That is my greatest desire," I replied. "If I can get a job at the mill I will not be going any farther than Cornwall and I will settle here, paying you, of course, that is, if you would want to have me as a boarder."

The chimes sounded midnight, and still we chattered on. I never would have believed it would be so sweet to be welcomed into the bosom of a loving family.

The next day, Mr. Sigouin returned from the mill saying, "I got a job to get you started at the mill. The work involves unwinding and carding the ends of cotton left on the bobbins so that they can be reused to make the coarse fabric used for making pockets. It's not difficult."

The whole first day I was on trial; I was so afraid of not doing my work as it should be done. But many times over the course of the day, my boss, Mr. Padus, told me, "I've never had anyone as adept at making *féline* as you." That's the name of the type of fibers my work produced.

I kept this employment, which I liked very much, and remained with the good Sigouin family for fifteen months, until November 1878. Then production was cut in half, and over the winter the whole operation stopped. I was temporarily laid off with the assurance that I would be rehired the following spring.


SOUTHWOOD

Finding myself out of work, I decided to spend the winter in the forests of New York State, in Southwood, some fifty miles* south of Ogdensburg. Once again, I left the good family, but this time separation was not as painful because we said, "*Au-revoir* (see you soon)" and not, "*Adieu* (goodbye)."

*I found a Southwood, NY near Syracuse about 100 miles south of Ogdensburg.

Alas! How little we know what the future will bring, even the near future. It's for the best this way, because how could we bear both the pains of the present and those of the future at the same time?

I got a job with a Mr. Hogwere and drove a Mr. John Jasmay's horses. We passed through Prescott and Ogdensburg, New York. In this last place, we obtained lodgings at a Canadian's home. That evening while we were chatting about one thing and another by the glow of the stove, I told him my life's story and asked if he knew of anyone named Marin.

"No, he replied, but I see a lot of people around here and I will be able to get some information for you. Don't forget to stop by when you are passing through this spring, maybe I'll have news for you."

These words didn't give me much hope; I had fully decided not to take to the road again in search of my parents. "But," I told myself, "it doesn't cost much to ask."

All winter long we were busy collecting pine bark. Over the summer when the sap rises, pine bark gets taken off the trees, on mountaintops, on valley floors, and in some truly impossible places; it all has to wait for the winter snows in order to be transported to the tanneries. We would gather the bark into bundles as big as some granaries. The four tanneries would consume up to eight cords of pine bark a day.

I very nearly left my feet in these mountains, these poor feet which froze for the third time—please God, let this be the last time! One of my wagon wheels got caught on a stump. I jumped down to see what was the matter and found myself standing in fifteen inches or so of water. It took a long time to return to camp

*Le Monde illustré*, 15 April 1893. Courtesy of BAnQ.

## Timber and Tanneries

By the early 19th century, Canada's and upstate New York's forests, abundant in tannin-rich hemlock and spruce, were exploited in the new timber and tanning industries. Quebec continued to use bark tannin to cure hides until 1910 while elsewhere tanneries switched to chrome, which worked faster but was far more polluting.

As Pierre explained, bark used for tannin was easier to take off hemlocks and spruce in the spring and summer when the sap flowed, but waited for easier transportation by sleigh over snow and iced trails in the winter months. Trees, on the other hand, were easier to cut in winter months when the sap didn't flow. Throughout most of the nineteenth century, workers cut trees, transported logs, and gathered and transported bark for tanneries in the winter months.

The lumber industry also took advantage of the availability of cheap, seasonal laborers in the winter months, like farmers who wanted to earn extra cash, or workers like Pierre who were laid off from mill work. This winter work was as dangerous as it was hard. Besides the threat of injuries from felling trees with axes, workers ran the daily risks of frostbite and falling through the ice as Pierre experienced. They lived in lumber camps, in cabins with central fireplaces like the ones shown below.[*]

*Canada Hall, The Timber Industry, Canadian Museum of Civilization Corporation

Exterior and interior of lumber camp cabin, *L'Opinion publique,* 18 May 1882 & 5 Feb. 1870. Courtesy of BAnQ.

and it was extremely cold. In the end, I got frostbite. The boss talked about sending me to a neighboring village until I healed.

"Please," I said, "keep me here. Where do you want me to go? I have no friends or relatives in this country. I will try not to be a burden. I'll pay you for your trouble."

They took pity on me and let me stay at the camp but they also took three-quarters of my pay. At this rate, it would take me a while to get rich.

In the beginning of March, there was a lot of rain and the men were laid off. I didn't forget to stop by the hotelkeeper in Ogdensburg. He had made a great number of inquiries, but they didn't amount to anything. However, while I was in Ogdensburg, I happened to cross paths with two of my brothers and three of my sisters, the eldest of whom was my Godmother, Justine.[49] But my name Marin prevented any possibility of recognition.

MY SECOND STAY IN
CORNWALL

I was so looking forward to going back to Mr. Sigouin's.

I found him dead! His body was laid out on boards. Burial and a funeral service were to take place the following day. When I arrived, the family's crying and sobbing redoubled. This unexpected death hit me like a bolt of lightning. I remained stunned and bewildered for months. I had found a father and now I lost him! For the second time, I became an orphan.

49. Most of these siblings in Ogdensburg were actually Pierre's half siblings from his father's first marriage. Justine Cholet's name appears on Pierre's baptismal record, see p. 4.

Mrs. Sigouin found herself in financial difficulties. She had to sell her house and move with her girls into an apartment elsewhere. I went to board at Mr. Robidoux's; he was a good man whom I had known since my first days in Cornwall. From time to time, I visited Mrs. Sigouin, whom I regarded as my mother, and her young daughters whom I called my sisters. It was always a pleasure for us to see each other, but now deprived of a husband and a father so much of the former joy and spontaneous gaiety would never return to this bereaved family.

I stayed at Mr. Robidoux's place for two years and three months while working at the mill. They treated me very well there, but I had become sad and dreamy. I was losing a lot of weight; I was visibly wasting away. Shut up in my small room, I often spent sleepless nights. I had no desire to start out again in search of my parents. I had gotten fed up with that vocation; but I found myself weighed down by discouragement and disgust. I had nourished so many high hopes and they had all gone up in smoke. I moved like a stranger in the world. During the whole course of my life, I had had only two years of happiness; then death had come to spread its shroud of sadness and isolation over my existence.

"Never, never again," I told myself through my tears, "will I be able to see those who gave me life."

Though I never suspected it, I *was* on the verge of finding them. Might my ill-defined malaise have been a vague premonition of the happiness that awaited me? As always, when my life had become too burdensome, I sought solace in the silence and stillness of the tomb.

# 8

## *Finding My Parents*

WHEN I LEAST
EXPECTED IT

Since the spring, a young girl about twenty-two years old, named Matilde Gauthier, worked at the same place and boarded with me at Mr. Robidoux's. Her parents lived in St.-Raphael parish, in Lancaster's eighth concession, consequently, not far from the border of Quebec Province and St.-Polycarpe parish. She got me to tell her my history and listened attentively. Several times she asked me to repeat certain events in my story that she had forgotten; she seemed extremely interested.

In August, Miss Gauthier went home to visit her family. They asked her, "Does Mr. Robidoux have many boarders?"

"Six: three women and three men. I feel very sorry for one of the men. He was kidnapped from home when he was about five years old, along with a younger brother who was four and a cousin of about six. He has been searching for his parents in the north, in the south, the east and west—all over—but with no success. He has given up. But alone at night, he often cries. Really, it's so sad to see him like that."

"About how old is this man?" asked Mrs. Gauthier.

"Around forty years old."

"The way you tell this story, it almost sounds like the brother of Mrs. Isidore Hamelin, the daughter of Mr. Hyacinthe Cholet of St.-Polycarpe."

"True," the girl replied, "now that you've made me think about it, I think he resembles him a lot.

"Well," the mother said to her children, "Mr. Hamelin left yesterday with his wife to visit his father-in-law; he is returning tomorrow. Watch out for him going by and we'll stop him."

Mr. and Mrs. Hamelin lived in the same concession a couple of miles farther on. The next day, when they were riding back at a gentle pace, Mrs. Gauthier ran out to the road calling out, "Mr. Hamelin, please stop so I can talk to you." She asked about some people living in Lower Canada and about Mr. Cholet and his wife. Mr. Hamelin replied that they were all in good health. "Now I'll come to the question," said Mrs. Gauthier. "You can't imagine why I stopped you. Mrs. Hamelin, didn't you lose a brother? I seem to recall having heard that."

"Unfortunately, not just one, but two, with a young cousin. We've heard no news, not a word about them since their disappearance."

At once, Mrs. Gauthier told them what her daughter had reported from Cornwall.

"Really," replied Mrs. Hamelin, "this story corresponds perfectly with the kidnapping of my brothers. I very much want to see this man, especially when you tell me he resembles me."

"It's a shame that my harvest is not yet finished or I would go at once to find him," broke in Mr. Hamelin.

"If you want," said Mrs. Gauthier, "my husband, who has to take Mathilde back to Cornwall next week, will bring him back."

"Certainly, and we will be very grateful"

Mrs. Hamelin was elated by the news, and Mrs. Gauthier was very happy to be the first to tell her.

## A RAY OF HOPE

A few days later, Mr. Gauthier and his daughter arrived at Mr. Robidoux's around noontime. This was the beginning of September. As he entered, he asked, "Where is the lost child?"

"At work."

"Will he be home soon?"

"Would he ever be late for his midday meal? But what do you have to tell him that is so urgent?"

"Well, you see, we have found his parents!"

Just as he said that, I was coming in.

"Wait, here he is."

"Good. I'm going to hide in the other room. Don't tell him, keep chatting with him for a while, I want to surprise him!"

"Come in, Louis, come in," said Mr. Robidoux. "Quick, quick come to the table so that I can read your fortune in the tea leaves."[50]

50. "*Tiré au thé*, to predict the future with the remains of the tea leaves left in the bottom of the cup after the infusion is drunk." —J.-B. Proulx.

This speech coming from Mr. Robidoux surprised me. He was a serious and unbending man whom I had never seen joking.

"Hurry up then," chimed in the other boarders, "hurry and drink your tea so that he can tell you where your parents are."

I found their behavior odd, very out of the ordinary. Mrs. Robidoux was coming and going. She circled around me, all the while wiping her eyes with the corner of her apron.

"Madam, you're crying!"

"Yes," she said, "I'm crying with happiness for you."

I understood nothing.

Just then Mr. Gauthier stepped in from the adjoining room and said, "My dear Sir, would you like to come with me? I am going to take you straight to your father!"

"Sir," I replied, "thank you very much for your kind offer. But if it is true that my father exists, I've been chasing after him for a long time. Let it now be his turn to take the trouble to come to see me.

"Ah ha," my table companions laughed, "you've gotten real independent."

"It's just that I can't get it into my head that my parents could be so near, when I have searched so far and wide."

"It doesn't matter, it's worth taking a chance one more time."

"Absolutely not, all too often, just when everything seemed certain, my useless searches led me to lose some good jobs. Now that I have one that suits me, I'm going to keep it."

"You can leave," said Mr. Robidoux, "and I promise you won't lose out. When you want to return, you will find your place kept warm for you. I will speak to the boss for you."

As I knew that Mr. Robidoux had a lot of influence at the mill, I was reassured.

"Thank you," I said. "On your guarantee, I'm leaving."

An hour later, I was in the wagon. Everyone, laughing and with beaming expressions, wished me good luck; they seemed happy for my hopes.

## TO MY FATHER'S HOUSE

About halfway there, we slept at the home of Mrs. Robidoux's father. The road seemed endless. I asked about my father and mother, their ages, their means of support.

"I have known for quite some time," Mr. Gauthier told me, "that your real name is not Louis Marin, but Pierre Cholet. Your father's name is Hyacinthe Cholet, and your cousin was named Pierre Doucet; his nickname was Cayen."

"In fact," I replied, "I have a slight recollection that one day on the ship someone said to us, 'From now on, you will be called Pierre Marin; you, Louis Marin; and you, Toussaint Marin.'"

"That makes sense," observed Mr. Gauthier. "Those men wished to erase any traces of your origins, and as you were raised at sea, they called you Marin."*

"And that's why," I added, "all my inquiries went nowhere, I was always knocking on the wrong doors."

We arrived at Mr. Hamelin's home by the afternoon of the next day. The house was built on a small hill, far from the road. We left the carriage down at the gate, and went up the hill on foot. When their children saw us coming, they clapped their hands and shouted, "Mama, here is Mr. Gauthier with our Uncle Polycarpe."

*Marin means "sailor" in French.

Polycarpe is the youngest of my brothers. It seems that we are the same height, have the same appearance, and the same gait. Without knowing it, the children, ages five and six, just gave favorable testimony to my identity.

On hearing the sound of my voice, my sister had a seizure and fell down, almost in a faint. My brother-in-law came outside and said, "Please don't come in just yet, my wife isn't feeling well, the excitement is too much for her."

He led us a short distance away to a shady area behind the barn. There seated on a big pine log, I began telling them my story from the beginning. My audience was first Mr. Gauthier, Mr. Hamelin, his hired hand, and soon my sister accompanied by a neighbor—both of whom remained hidden in the barn; but I heard them sighing, because they were crying the whole time.

I talked for two hours.

Mr. Hamelin said, "My friend, your story makes sense and you don't look like an impostor."

My sister came out of her hiding place and threw herself into my arms saying, "I accept you as my brother. You are, because as soon as I saw you I was overcome."

"Since you recognize me as your brother, take me to our parents. I will leave it to their judgment and go by what they say."

"With the greatest pleasure," said Mr. Hamelin, "but you will have to wait a few days. The rest of my grain is still on the ground and has to be brought in before I can leave; I wouldn't want to leave it out in the rain."

"My dear Sir, take all the time you need. I will be only too happy to help you with the harvest." I thanked Mr. Gauthier for having brought me.

My brother-in-law said to him, "Since it was you who discovered him, you should come with us to my father-in-law's, this happy occasion wouldn't be complete without you."

"Very well," Gauthier replied, "when you are ready to leave, just let me know. I have never refused a good outing."

I stayed three days at Mr. Hamelin's. When we returned from the fields at mealtimes, my sister enveloped me with kindness. She had never known me. She is younger than I, having been born in the autumn following my kidnapping. But my name was familiar to her; she had often heard our mother talking about the poor, little Pierre who had died. Already she had a fine family of her own: five boys and a girl. I refrained from talking about my misfortunes in front of her, as she would immediately start to cry. Every night, neighborhood people would gather to hear me tell of my adventures. Among those were two of my uncles: my mother's brother, Mr. Etienne St.-Amand, and Mr. Latrielle, married to Mr. St.-Amand's sister. Questions poured in from all sides, which I answered as best I could. No one doubted that I was Hyacinthe Cholet's son.

AT MY FATHER'S
HOUSE

On the fourth day, around eight in the morning, my sister, my brother-in-law, and I left in the same wagon for my father's house in Saint-Polycarpe. Along the way we picked up Mr. Gauthier and his wife, and my Uncle St.-Amand and my aunt. The three wagons followed one after the other raising clouds of dust. Everything was gay: our conversation, our Sunday finery, our dashing horses trotting with heads held high, the beautiful autumn sunlight casting a warm glow on us. People in the fields stopped working to watch us pass and seemed to be smiling at my good fortune.

My Uncle Latrielle had gone on ahead to alert my aged father and mother of our arrival. He was afraid that a sudden surprise would be bad for them. He arrived three hours before us.

"Hyacinthe," he said, "your boy who you thought was lost forever has come back."

"Which boy?"

"The oldest of the two you lost thirty years ago, Pierre!"

"And the other?"

"He is dead, as well as his cousin, little Cayen."

In a few words, my uncle told them about the kidnapping, my desertion and the long search. At first, the two old people thought it was a hoax. But Mr. Latrielle remained so serious. He repeated with such an air of authority, "I tell you, Hyacinthe, that your boy has been found, he is coming with Hamelin, and will be here in a couple of hours," that at last they let themselves be persuaded. Then they were overcome with joy. My mother wept; my father paced around the house. He went from window to window saying, "They haven't arrived yet. What are they doing? They're taking a lot of time."

Mr. Gauthier had talked to the others about me. "Let him be. Don't say anything to him when we arrive so we can see if he remembers anything."

Reaching the school house, which was a few hundred yards from my father's house, I said, "Stop, I've been to the school here four or five times."

They started to laugh. "You're guessing, you couldn't remember this school house because it has since been rebuilt."

"It's not the building I remember, it's the cross. It was blessed the year I was stolen. I remember very well when the priest came for the ceremony and preached a sermon from the top of a stump."

This cross was an upright cedar with only its branches lopped off, onto which was attached a crosspiece for the arms. These dormant memories sprang back to life when I found myself again at the places where they occurred. "That is true," said my Uncle St.-Amand, "the cross was blessed around that time!"

We arrived at about five o'clock in the evening. Already, news of my return had spread through the neighborhood. Fifty or so people had assembled in and around the house. I waited until the horses were tethered before entering. It upset me to see so many people. I entered by the kitchen door. Not a sound could be heard in the crowd; all eyes were upon me; I felt very ill at ease. Someone pushed a chair near a small table over to me. I sat down.

My mother came towards me. Leaning on the table with both hands for support, she said in a faltering voice, "Is it really true... that you had . . . been kidnapped?"

With these words, she started to totter; she was about to collapse when several women caught her and gently took her to sit on a sofa. I went outside, I was suffocating; I needed to breathe some fresh air. Someone brought me cold water; I washed my face and felt better. My mother regained her senses. This unexpected incident moved the whole assembly. The men broke into small groups and chatted quietly; the women wept.

I came back in; they led me to the main room of the house. My father put his arms around my neck and warmly embraced me several times. "My poor child," he said, "tell us what happened to you, tell us from the beginning."

141

Everyone sat down; the room was completely packed, and the crowd outside was steadily swelling, heads pressed against windowpanes, mouths closed, ears open.

"Dear father, dear mother, dear relatives, never has it given me so much pleasure to tell my story. But I can hardly talk, I am too emotional.

"Take your time," someone said, "take your time."

I spoke for two hours. I took advantage of the occasional interruptions of the women's sobbing to catch my breath.

Then my father, patting my arms, my face and hair, taking my hands in his, said, "Is it really you, Pierre, is it really true that you have returned. Say it, is it really you?"

My mother was also in front of me—I can still see her—her two elbows resting on her knees, regarding me with love and affection.

At eight o'clock we got up to stretch a bit.

Everyone was saying, "*C'est lui*, it's him!"

"Yes," replied my father, "it's my son, my Pierre. I recognize him as the child I have cried over for so long.

"Listen, I said, "as a last proof I will tell you about the marks we had on us. Pierre Doucet had a small lump on his head, Toussaint had two scars from smallpox on his left temple, and I also have two pockmarks on my right groin."

"That's true," said my mother, "He could not have guessed these hidden things. What better proof do we need? I have no doubt the good Lord has returned our son."

"Yes," replied my father, "the good Lord has loved us today, let us give thanks."

At these words everyone fell to their knees and recited the rosary aloud.

The strangers left and only relatives and close neighbors re-mained. There were about thirty of us at the table to eat the fatted calf (among those present was my cousin Elie Doucet, a theology student who died a few years later as a priest). After supper, the celebration began; the young people danced to violin music until midnight.

Like the father of the prodigal son, mine said, "All's well, enjoy yourselves. Our child was lost, he is found again, he was dead, now he is returned to the living."

OFFICIAL

RECOGNITION

The sun has its spots, a beautiful day its clouds. In general, ev-erybody believed me. Only one brother,[51] the one to whom my parents had chosen to leave their farm in return for a pension, had some doubts.

He told them over and over again, "Be careful, don't rush into anything, you may be dealing with a con artist who wants to swin-dle you out of your possessions (*butin*)."[52]

These words made them apprehensive.

I spoke to my brother, "Have no fear, Sir, I'm not going to hurt anyone, nor will I claim any part of the inheritance. All that I ask is for the right to call the authors of my existence my father and my

51. This brother, named Hyacinthe Cholet, was eight months old when Pierre was kidnapped in 1845. Pierre and Toussaint also had an older sister as well as probably three half siblings (who later moved to Ogdensburg) living at the family home at the time of the kidnapping.

52. "In Canada, *butin* [spoils, loot, plunder] is often used in the sense of goods [*biens*], possessions." —J.-B. Proulx

143

mother, because in reality that's what they are, and finally I've the good fortune to have found them again."

My father remained quiet and a certain malaise hung over the household.

The next day after dinner, my father said, "Would you like us to go together to see the pastor and find out what he thinks of our situation?"

"Certainly," I replied. "Take all the precautions you want. For you it's a matter of being prudent, for me it's the fulfillment of my dreams." I said the truth; I could only gain from my story being subjected to the test of a trial.

On seeing the three of us enter his office, the pastor showed us to our seats and said, "What's new, Father Cholet?"

"The news, father, is that a great miracle has happened."

"What is it?"

"I have found my son who has been lost for thirty-five years! Here he is."

The pastor listened to me for a long time in silence, asked me a few questions, and at the end said without equivocation, "I have no reason to doubt the truthfulness of this good man; moreover, he resembles you a great deal. You could perhaps go and see Mr. Lanthier, explain your troubles to him, and put your trust in his decision with complete confidence."

Mr. Jacques Lanthier was the representative of Soulanges County in the Federal Chamber. He was a man of experience and good judgment, respected by everyone. He was working in his yard when we arrived; his wife called him in.

On entering, he came over to shake our hands, saying, "Bonjour, Messieurs Cholet."

My father replied, "Who told you that this young man is a Cholet?"

"Who told me?…but… I believe I know all your children… family resemblance at least, if I cannot distinguish them all by their baptismal names."

"And so you find that this one here has a family resemblance?"

"Without a doubt! What? Isn't he one of your boys?"

"Yes, at least I think so, but he's not the one who you think."

And so we began once again the long exposition and examination of our case.

In the middle of this, Mrs. Lanthier, who had overheard everything, entered the room saying, "Are you one of the three Marin boys that the papers talked about a few years ago?"

"Yes Madam, Marin was my name back then."

She pulled from a stack of newspapers an issue from ten years ago and read the notice I had placed in Montreal. I was glad for this incident; her newspaper just confirmed one of my claims and by a kind of ricochet effect lent credence to my other assertions.

When he had heard and weighed everything, Mr. Lanthier expressed himself as follows: "Mr. Cholet, go away satisfied. There is no doubt that this man is your son. All told, his history, his age, his resemblance to you, what he says about his youth, the hidden marks he showed you, his entire story seems candid and truthful. If you can't recognize him as your son, don't keep searching for another."

"Thank you, Mr. Lanthier. Ever since his arrival, I never for a moment doubted that God wished to console me in my old age with my son. But your words reassure me. Come, my dear, let us enjoy our good fortune."

We went by the church, to thank God for having restored at long last a son to his parents. Our hearts were full of gratitude. We hadn't realized how long we had prayed. The sun was setting behind the treetops when we left for home, happy, content, and light-hearted. To express the fullness of our feelings, we needed only to say, "God is good!"

I added, "The Blessed Virgin surely brought me back. If you only knew how many times she protected me in my many perils."

"As for me," said my mother, "ever since you were gone, not a single night passed that I did not pray for my lost children."

Thank you, dear God, may your Holy Name be forever blessed.


## CONCLUSION

The reader, who has had the patience to follow my story thus far, may be interested to know what has happened to me since. This curiosity is only natural, so I will add a few closing words.

I stayed for about a month at the family home, in its gentle and loving atmosphere that was new to me; I could hardly believe it was real. Every morning on waking up, I would say to myself, "Another beautiful day!" I never tired of the endless conversations with my good family and of being able to call them by those sweet names: mother, father, sister and brother.

In October, since I didn't want to add to their expenses or to be regarded as lazy, I went back to work at the mill in Cornwall. I was touched to the bottom of my heart to see how much the Robidoux family and especially Mrs. Sigouin and her girls shared in my happiness. Fifteen days later one of my brother's, who lived in Ogdensburg and whom I had never met, came to get me and

take me to his home. In this city, as I said before, I had still another brother and three other sisters. Coddled, spoiled, pampered,
I spent the fall staying with one, then another of them. Among
them, my Godmother Justine, especially, didn't want me to leave.

On New Year's Day, I returned to the family home for the
first time since reaching the age of reason to ask for the paternal
blessing, to eat the customary bread, and to receive my New Year's
gift. Having gone to visit my brother-in-law Hamelin, the rector of
Saint-Raphael church engaged me as a sexton. In 1882 just before
Lent, I gave up the single life to marry a young woman of twenty-
two, Anna Levac. God's blessing descended on our household and
we have a baby girl who is now fifteen months old.

For three years I rang Saint-Raphael's church bell. Thinking
to make a good change of jobs, I exchanged that bell for another
at the church of Sainte-Anne de Prescott. But in this new parish, a sexton's job paid even less. I quit in March 1886 in order to
look around in this wide universe for better paying work. My wife
spent the year that just ended boarding at one of my brothers in
St.-Polycarpe.

My book is finished, but my life goes on. If I take after my family, I will not be turning over the last page too soon. My mother is
seventy years old and takes care of her house like a young girl; my
father who is eighty-eight takes great pleasure in walking to Mass
on a beautiful summer day——and he lives three miles from church.
I had been deprived of these dear parents for so many long years,
may the good Lord let me keep them for a long time to come!

# AFTERWORD

$T$hough life in rural nineteenth century Canada revolved around family, farm and parish, Pierre Cholet never acquired a farm. His determined pursuit to find his parents led him to lose at least two possibilities of gaining his own land. The first opportunity was presented by the childless, elderly Marins in Gloucester when Cholet was thirty or thirty-one years old. Mr. Marin said he might give Cholet his farm in return for a pension if he stayed on, but Cholet declined his offer. The second and more likely opportunity was with the Sigouin family in Castor when Cholet was thirty-five years old. The Sigouins had seven daughters but no sons to help with the farm work. After living with the Sigouins and working on their farm for a year, he decided to move on and work elsewhere, "I committed the folly of leaving a place where I was so well off. It is said that each life has an evil hour; this was mine" (107). When he return several months and several calamities later, he learned that without his labor the Sigouins had had to sell their land. Thus Cholet lost his last chance of getting land.

Meanwhile, his parents, believing their two eldest sons long dead, had already given their farm to their third son Hyacinthe in return for a pension. This son immediately doubted the identity of Pierre who returned as a propertyless stranger. So, like the story of the sixteenth century Basque peasant Martin Guerre, made famous in the 1983 film "Return of Martin Guerre" starring Gerard Depardieu, Pierre Cholet had to prove to his own family that he was not an impostor. In Chapter 1, J.-B. Proulx informed the reader that he himself had taken pains to establish the validity of Pierre Cholet's story and identity.

WHAT HAPPENED TO PIERRE CHOLET in the years following the completion of his book in 1887? Cholet, who had so widely traveled around the world and all over eastern Canada, chose to remain near his parents in St.-Polycarpe, never moving farther than some twenty-five to thirty miles away in eastern Ontario around Cornwall. Sadly, documents reveal that his baby daughter died on July 30, 1887 only a few months after his book was completed. Two years later his wife died at the age of twenty-nine. They had no other surviving children. The 1901 Ontario census, which recorded Pierre Cholet as a widower, reported that the sixty-year-old Pierre Cholet (now spelled Cholette) was working full-time as a carpenter earning about $200 a year, that he spoke some English, and boarded with the Bissonette family in Charlottenburg Township, Glengarry County, near Cornwall. Pierre Cholet did not remarry.

Though death came again "to spread its shroud of sadness and isolation" over his life (as it had with Mr. Sigouin's sudden death in 1879), Pierre Cholet apparently did not again seek "the silence and stillness of the tomb" (131). According to Cholette family lore, Pierre Cholet had many friends who came to visit him and he remained close to several of his many relatives. Very likely he remained close to the Sigouin family who lived around Cornwall as he did. Pierre Cholet's book made him famous in francophone Canada, and he undoubtedly had many visitors requesting him to recount episodes of his thirty-six-year-long journey from his kidnapping to his return.

In 1978, Dr. Albert Cholette, a ninety-three-year-old relative of Pierre Cholet's, recalled his mother telling him stories about his famous relative and later meeting him in person around 1895.

> ...several years later around the age of ten or twelve, I met the hero of the story Pierre Cholet at the home of one of my father's brothers Ferdinand Cholette, who was a tailor and a barber at Sainte-Anne-de-Prescott. Despite the passage of time, I can clearly recall that Pierre Cholet, who was then around fifty-five years old, had a strong presence. His speech still retained traces of a French accent acquired during his long stay in France.
>
> Naturally, I pressed him with questions about his big adventure. He told me about one of the sad episodes of his exile, during his life at sea: about his escape from the French frigate while it was in the port of St. Jean, especially, after this first escape with his brother when they were recaptured and punished with twenty whiplashes. Then he had me look at the scars that were still visible on his back.*

*Dr. Albert Cholette's Introduction to *L'Enfant perdu et retrouvé, ou, Pierre Cholet*, with illustrations by his daughter-in-law Suzanne Longtin-Cholette (Montreal: Fides, 1978).
Dr. Albert Cholette, who lived to be ninety-seven years old, happened to attend the same seminary, Séminaire de Ste. Therèse, as had the author J.-B Proulx and later studied medicine from 1904-11 at the same medical school of the University of Laval at Montreal that Proulx worked so hard to save when he was that university's Vice-Rector ten years earlier (see boxed text p. 9).

Pierre Cholet remained a vigorous man up to the time of his death. In the year he died, he carved and painted a wooden sign (shown below) both as an advertisement of himself as a house painter (*"pentre"*) and as a souvenir of his famous story. The fish he carved looks like a codfish (you can see its resemblance to the codfish pictured on the late nineteenth century two cents and the 1937 one cent Newfoundland stamps shown below). He reportedly died while painting a house on December 7, 1907 at the age of 67.

Dr. Cholette concisely explained in his introduction why the spelling of the family name changed from Cholet to Cholette: "I'll take this opportunity to tell you that with time the name Cholet, originally written with a single "t", was transformed into Cholette, as it is now pronounced."

THE READER MAY HAVE noticed a few minor inconsistencies in the text. In the letters Proulx received in Chapter 1, Pierre Cholet's father stated that Pierre returned thirty-five years later, in September 1880 at the age of forty. But using the careful dates of the text it is more probable that Pierre was reunited with his family a year later in September 1881. In another letter, Mrs. Isaie Hamelin said that it was Pierre's mother who angered the peddler. Pierre Cholet's own account put the blame on his cousin's mother Mrs. Doucet who happened to be visiting Mrs. Cholet when the peddler stopped by. Both versions reported the peddler saying, "You will remember me..."

There are only two even more minor discrepancies that genealogical researches of Jack Cholette have brought to light. In the conclusion, very likely written in May 1887, Pierre Cholet mentioned that his daughter was fifteen months old when she would have been a few months younger (she was born in April 1886) and he gave his father's age as eighty-eight when he would have been eighty-four. His father was born in 1803 and died in 1894 aged ninety. It is not known when Pierre Cholet's mother died.

In 1999, I briefly did some checking into maritime records for St. Malo for the relevant years 1854-1870 when Pierre Cholet and his brother were ship's boys and sailors. Unfortunately, I had only one afternoon to spend in the hall of records, located in Rennes so this research was far from complete. I was not able to find in the ship registers any records of Pierre Marin, Toussaint Marin or of Captain Cottin. Pierre Cholet never provided in his story the names of any of his ships, his ship company, or the school where he and his brother were raised in St. Malo. Moreover, "Marin," which means sailor, hardly seems a prudent name to give to kid-napped boys, bought by a sea captain and forced to become sailors. Maybe the ship company registered the kidnapped boys under different names, or maybe since Pierre Cholet jumped ship in war-time, he changed his false name as well as the captain's name in his story in order to protect his identity. Perhaps someone will one day clear up this mystery.

Many readers have expressed the desire for a longer version of Pierre Cholet's story, one that integrates the historical notes into the text and that paints the scenes and characters with more color and depth.

Please turn the page for the first chapter of an expanded Pierre Cholet novel coming out soon:

**THE TRUE ADVENTURES OF**

**PIERRE CHOLET**

# THE TRUE ADVENTURES OF PIERRE CHOLET

Pastor Jean-Baptiste Proulx was vexed to discover that the soft, persistent tapping was not coming from the intermittent and interminable construction work outside—new buildings were going up everywhere in the prosperous Montreal of the 1880s, and construction mania had even spread to his own building's courtyard. From his window he could see a section of the jury-rigged scaffolding, now graced with a new dusting of snow; every now and then one or two workmen bundled up against the cold and exhaling clouds of breath crossed into view. Someone was knocking on his office door.

Proulx's small office was located on the ground floor of the Asile Sainte-Darie at 182 Fullum Street in downtown Montreal. This large, three story brick building, built in the shape of a cross and topped with mansards, presently housed about one hundred fifty women: ninety-six female prisoners, a dozen female penitents, and thirty-two Sisters of the Good Shepherd. Ten years ago the first women prisoners had arrived to the newly built women's prison, founded and run by the Sisters of the Good Shepherd; the Sisters were now making further modifications and planning new additions. For the past two years, Proulx served as the Asile's chaplain.

He had begun the morning making his usual rounds of visits to prisoners and penitents. These visits with mostly sad and angry young women too long confined in their cold, austere cells when not performing chores or going to Mass always left him feeling depressed. Moreover, he felt not a little hypocritical in his role of persuading the young prisoners to resign themselves to their internment when he had recently escaped for several months to Europe. And the nuns were so frugal with many of life's necessities, like heat. True, they were habitually strapped for funds; they were even talking about putting the prisoners to work in the Asile's dank, dark basement as laundresses. For a moment, as he blew on his cold fingers, he wished he could exchange places with the workmen outside his window.

Since finishing his prison rounds, Proulx's bulky form had been hunched over a paper-strewn desktop. He planned to take advantage of the rest of the day free of appointments to catch up on outside work. As usual he had over-committed himself. It was the beginning of February 1886, and he was behind on finishing two books, both chronicles of his recent travels. A year ago, he had almost finished the first—travels with Monsignor Lorrain to missions in Hudson's Bay in the summer of 1884—when the formidable Curé Antoine Labelle invited Proulx to accompany him to Europe. This European tour grew into a five-month stay lasting until August 1885.

His notes and drafts of letters from the Hudson's Bay trip lay spread out before him, his outpourings scribbled on rocky summits, in the bottom of canoes, and in tents pitched in the deep forest wilderness. Engaged in organizing these diaristic accounts into final book form, his pen poised to cross out or write additional comments, Proulx ignored the knocking at the door. Instead, he contemplated the vast, majestic pine forests of Hudson's Bay and replayed in his mind's eye, now without terror, the death-defying canoe rides down the Rapide de l'Ile with Bishop Lorrain and the unflappable Abbitibien guides, especially the head guide Okouchin at the tiller.

But the knock did not cease as Proulx anticipated, it became more insistent. With a heavy sigh, he steeled himself for a short session with one of the sisters, probably Sister Agnes. His last encounter with Sister Agnes had been less than pleasant. Maybe harboring some resentment of his lengthy absence in Europe, she had ended their tense conversation without a smile, saying, "Your restless energy doesn't seem suited to our community. Perhaps you feel too restricted here." He had to admit that her parting remark, while not sympathetic, was not unjust. Nevertheless, it left a lingering sting.

So he was both surprised and relieved to find a stranger at the door: a man with a hat in one hand and a bundle of papers in the other, looking somewhat abashed. Like Proulx, he was of medium height and middle aged—a trifle taller than Proulx's five foot six inches, maybe a few years older than Proulx's forty years, and definitely slimmer. His face was handsome if still somewhat boyish: small, regular features set in a broad, tanned face. Most striking were the clear blue eyes framed by thick, dark lashes and well-defined eyebrows. Proulx surmised the man must have recently visited the barber's for his dark, wavy hair, lightly sprinkled with gray, was neatly trimmed and pomaded as was his moustache. Under the man's unbuttoned overcoat, Proulx observed a dark brown jacket, bow tie, and white shirt, none of it new or expensive, but well cared for. Clearly, the caller had gone to some pains for this visit, yet he didn't look like a tradesman or a center city Montrealais.

"Are you Father Jean-Baptiste Proulx who writes books? I've just been to see the publisher Mr. Beauchemin, and he told me to see you. I've come from St.-Polycarpe parish. My name is Pierre Cholet," the man finished breathlessly.

"I'm that Jean-Baptiste Proulx," he said kindly shaking Mr. Cholet's hand. "Come in and sit down." Almost reflexively he responded to the shy cry for help that he came across so often in his calling, and tried to put the man at his ease. "What can I do for you? First, where are you from, originally?" He had detected in the man's speech an accent that was more European than Canadian, and he was intrigued.

The man sat woodenly on the edge of his chair. He took a swift survey of Proulx's cramped office and cluttered desk. Shelves crammed with books, periodicals, correspondence, and miscellaneous papers occupied nearly all the available wall space. Among several maps and prints displayed on the wall, he spied a framed diploma from Sainte-Thérèse Seminary. Yes, Mr. Beauchemin had sent him to a man of letters alright. He took a deep breath and without further small talk launched into a concise summary of his life. This he delivered entirely in short sentences, as if he were well rehearsed at presenting his resume—which he was.

"I was born in 1840 in the parish of St.-Polycarpe. My father's name is Hyacinthe Cholet. I was kidnapped when I was five years old and taken across the ocean to St. Malo. I was forced to become a sailor on French merchant vessels. I spent my youth at sea. I finally deserted ship. I began a search all over Quebec for my family. After ten long years I found them. I have written out the story of my life;" he lifted his sheaf of papers. "I brought it to the publisher Mr. Beauchemin. He took a minute or two to look it over. He said he was interested in my story, but my writing wasn't ready for publication. He sent me to you. Could you polish it up for me?" He stopped as abruptly as he began, fixing his clear blue eyes on Proulx.

"Let me see your manuscript." Proulx's lively, dark eyes scanned the pages. His customary, high energy that he applied to everything he undertook now focused entirely on Cholet's writing. He ignored Cholet's frank stare and impatiently took up one page after another, sometimes returning to earlier pages. Gradually, his large but agreeable features changed from happy interest to puzzlement to frown. Cholet looked alternately hopeful and anxious.

Half an hour later, Proulx pushed his fingers through his thick, curly, black hair, similarly flecked with a few silvery strands, and exhaled noisily. Cracking his knuckles—one of his nervous habits employed when he didn't have a cigar in hand—he waited a bit to begin.

"Your story is really remarkable and original," he began gently. "It has potential!" He paused while searching for the right diplomatic formulation. "But, unfortunately, Mr. Beauchemin is right; your story needs a little more work, more… ugh…, more filling out. It seems you have many exciting adventures to relate, some sad, tragic events and some amusing ones, too, in here. Take for instance the shipwreck you describe, too many details are missing. But without more details, more description, the body of your text is like a…, a skeleton, a tantalizing skeleton," Proulx smiled. "From what I've read so far, your account is full of gaps. You haven't developed the events in your story sufficiently." Proulx's large, mobile features reddened and appeared to take on an angry cast, although his bright, brown eyes remained friendly. Proulx flipped through the manuscript again and finally looked up to see a stricken-looking Pierre Cholet.

He tried to soften his criticisms. "Mr. Cholet, you have presented just the bare bones of a good story. They need more muscle and fleshing out. This is a problem common to all inexperienced writers. They either forget that the reader doesn't know anything about their story or they think the reader would be bored by details that are themselves hard to sort out. So they skip over them, when it's precisely in these carefully developed and organized details that a story comes to life."

Without a word, Mr. Cholet slowly and stiffly gathered up his pages. When all was neatly retied, he pushed the manuscript away as if it were an alien object and shrugged. "I can tell you all the details you want about that shipwreck and anything else. I can remember all the events of my life: my kidnapping, my life at sea, my shipwrecks—I was shipwrecked not once but twice, my searches for my long lost family through the towns and countryside of Quebec, all as if they happened yesterday."

Clenching his fists, he stood up abruptly, and moved around the desk seeking in the cramped office space a place to pace. Cholet suddenly looked more robust and vigorous than he had at first appeared. With growing apprehension, Proulx watched him move about. "I have regaled friends and relatives, neighbors and strangers from all over Quebec for many hours, even for days at a time, with my stories. Everyone has begged me to write down my adventures for them and for their children, to get them into a book. But whenever I picked up a pen... it's as if I hoisted sail only to lose the wind and to be left with so many useless sails flapping, like these pages here. Put a pen and paper into my hands and I'm like a ship's boy lost in the rigging. I have spent so much time struggling to write good, correct French, yet these pages here are only fit for…for… oakum. Caulking," he amended on seeing Proulx's puzzled look. Almost theatrically, his posture slumped. He turned sad, hangdog eyes on Proulx. "Could you help me polish up these pages and put them into book form, Father?"

Proulx struggled with contradictory feelings, his generous impulses warring against his better judgment. He liked this man's story, at least the bare bones of it, a Canadian who struggled for most of his life to return to his roots in the Canadian countryside. He impulsively wanted to help Mr. Cholet, but practically he realized that he would have to devote hours and hours of work to make it publishable. Meanwhile, he was so far behind on his own writing projects. Unable to reach a decision, he remained silent.

"You want to hear more about my first shipwreck?" Mr. Cholet implored. Without waiting for an answer, his posture straightened and he began. "Only sixteen days out from St. Malo— after a smooth sail across the Atlantic—our frigate entered the Bay of St. Lawrence. We were nearing our first port of call, Pictou. Then, in no time, the sky went from a light, hazy blue to blue black, the wind backed to the southwest, and a thick bank of fog rolled in. The temperature dropped faster than a gull diving for chum. Now our teeth were chattering and we couldn't see more than a few feet in front of us. My brother Toussaint and I heard the sailors shouting, 'There's rocks ahead. Look out for the rocks!' We all scrambled to carry out the captain's next commands but it was too late!…"

Proulx was struck by the transformation. When he was seated at Proulx's desk confronting the efforts of his own writing, Cholet had seemed to shrink into himself. Now on his feet and retelling his story anew, he shed his diffidence and became an expansive and captivating raconteur, even eloquent. His performance was an oddly compelling mixture of the Canadian countryside and of Europe, of speech riddled with apt Quebec expressions and delivered in a European accent. His lively gestures and facial expressions with light blue eyes under dancing eyebrows, now arching, now furrowing added to the colorful impression .

Proulx offered a cigar to Mr. Cholet, who declined it. While taking a moment to clip the end of his cigar and light it, Proulx thought about the possibilities of Mr. Cholet's story; this would be a stretch for him. He emerged from his cigar-lighting ritual to find Cholet's fretful eyes on him, his dark eyebrows knitted.

"Mr. Cholet, I haven't rejected your story. Leave your manuscript with me. Give me more time to look it over and we'll see." Cholet's eyebrows relaxed and the clouds scuttled off his face. He heartily shook Proulx's hand on leaving and, thanking him profusely, secured a return visit in a few weeks time.

Pierre Cholet seemed to sweep the air and space out with him. Alone again, Proulx felt the walls of his cramped office press in. He leaned back in his chair, folded his hands over his ample waist, and mulled over the folly of taking on another writing project. Frowning, he puffed on his cigar, gazed out his window, and caught sight of Cholet's retreating figure silhouetted against the snow. He watched Cholet amble out of the Asile's courtyard in what Proulx fancied to be a sailor's gait. "Definitely more a man of the outdoors than one who sits too long at a desk as I do these days. Ah well, *revenons à nos moutons*, let's get back to work." He picked up a page of his notes and his pen with a flourish. As the firs and mists of Hudson's Bay moved in, the walls of his office cell receded.

CPSIA information can be obtained at www.ICGtesting.com
Printed in the USA
LVOW10s1749101014

408244LV00001B/76/A

9 780615 150819